The Ultimate TV Game Show Book

Volume I

The Ultimate TV

Los Angeles

Game Show Book

Volume I

By
Steve Ryan
and
Fred Wostbrock

With a tribute to Bill Cullen

09   08   07   06   05   5   4   3   2   1

Library of Congress Cataloging-in-Publication Data

Ryan, Steve.
    The ultimate TV game show book / Steve Ryan and Fred Wostbrock.
       p. cm.
    Includes bibliographical references and index.
    1. Game shows—United States—Miscellanea. I. Wostbrock, Fred. II. Title.

PN1992.8.Q5R93 2004
791.45'6—dc22
ISBN 1-5662-291-1   2004009611

Printed in the United States of America

Volt Press
A division of Bonus Books
9255 Sunset Blvd.,
Suite 717
Los Angeles, CA 90069

TABLE OF CONTENTS

Bob Eubanks

Here we see *PowerBall* host Bob Eubanks and Steve Ryan playing contestant in a rehearsal for "Zero Gravity," one of Steve's game creations. The same technology that makes airplanes fly (the Bernoulli effect) was used to levitate the huge ball over the rotating wheel. Contestants' lives were changed forever when the ball came to rest in the $1,000,000 space.

Foreword

I've had the pleasure of working with both Fred and Steve over the years, and it's a delight for me to introduce their latest book. But first, let me tell you a little about the authors.

In 1978, an eighteen-year-old young man walked up to me at a mall in Paramus, New Jersey, and gave me a collage of my career up to that time. He was a walking encyclopedia of game show trivia. I found out later that he collected pictures of game show hosts the way that most teenagers collected baseball cards. Anything I could think of to ask him about game shows, he knew the answer. The young man's name is Fred Wostbrock. Life takes some very unusual turns. One of my biggest fans is now my agent.

I had the opportunity to work with Steve Ryan, first in 1984 on the Goodson game show *Trivia Trap* and most recently on the *PowerBall* lottery game show, where Steve's fertile mind created many of the games.

Together, Fred and Steve are a dynamic writing team and really know game shows inside and out. You might already be familiar with their chronicled world of game shows through *The Encyclopedia of TV Game Shows.* Here, they have written the definitive history of game show trivia. They have even unearthed a photograph of me introducing the Beatles in Los Angeles back in 1964 when I was a disc jockey at KRLA radio. This marvelous book includes many great visuals of me, my peers, and my hero, Bill Cullen. What you are about to read is an amazing collection of known and unknown facts about one of America's traditional forms of entertainment.

Bob Eubanks

Bob Eubanks

A Tribute to Bill Cullen

Rare is an individual who finds a cozy niche. The spinning wheel of fortune was good to one William Lawrence Cullen. We lost beloved Bill on July 7, 1990, at the age of seventy. His track record was quite impressive; no television performer before or since has equaled his longevity: 25,000 radio and television shows between 1939 and 1988, when he retired.

Bill was so popular during the late sixties that he was appearing on all three networks. He graced the cover of the national *TV Guide* seven times … twice in one month! The collegiate-looking Cullen, with horn-rimmed glasses and a big smile, appeared on more than thirty-five network radio and television programs, beginning as an announcer but quickly becoming popular as a master of ceremonies. There is not one year between 1946 and 1988 that Bill Cullen wasn't on the radio airwaves or on the television screen. His sharp ad-libbing abilities, breezy style, and familiar voice always brought a sense of comfort to game show fans of all ages.

Born on the south side of Pittsburgh on February 18, 1920, Bill became intrigued with radio at an early age. His first break came in 1938 when he was hired at local radio station WWSW, earning $35 a week. He eventually became a sports announcer in 1939 and earned $500 a week. In 1944, he packed his one suitcase and moved from Pittsburgh to New York City. The young kid from Pittsburgh was soon to become the "Dean of Game Show Emcees." In 1946 he landed his first emcee job on CBS radio wheedling answers from contestants on *Winner Take All.* The principal winner was Cullen, who springboarded his career at CBS. In 1948, he was the obvious choice to host *Winner Take All* when it hit the TV airwaves. Bill was a natural, and the rest, as we say, is history. A few of his shows from 1949 to 1956 were *Act It Out, Give and Take, The Bill Cullen Show, Bank on the Stars, Name That Tune,* and these two classics, *I've Got a Secret* and *The Price Is Right.*

Cullen first appeared on *I've Got a Secret* in 1952, and he remained as a panelist for the show's entire fifteen-year run. While appearing on *I've Got a Secret,* Cullen also hosted his own morning radio show, *Pulse,* over at WNBC radio. Debuting in 1955, the show became number one within a few months and stayed there for nearly six years.

In 1956 Cullen was named host of *The Price Is Right,* a Bob Stewart–created show for Goodson and Todman Productions. Bill and Bob Stewart would develop a lifelong friendship and work relationship that would delight American TV viewers for decades to come. The dynamic duo gave us these game show favorites: *Eye Guess, Three on a Match, The $25,000 Pyramid, Winning Streak, Blankety Blanks, Pass the Buck, The Love Experts,* and *Chain Reaction. The Price Is Right,* which began the relationship, was so successful that it was number one in both daytime and prime time for years.

Maintaining an exhausting pace through much of the fifties and sixties, Bill was on the air twenty-five and a half hours each week—a record that has yet to be broken. At times Bill was hosting shows on both the East Coast and West Coast, commuting more than 5,000 miles a week … he never missed a show, which contributed to his solid reputation as a superb emcee. Along the way he met Ann Macomber, sister-in-law to Jack Narz, who was pleased to introduce the two on October 1, 1954. For over a year, they had a once-a-week date and many transcontinental telephone calls. On December 24, 1955, Ann and Bill were wed. A true love story!

As the seventies approached the famous Bill Cullen crew cut had grown out and the familiar horn-rimmed glasses were replaced with modish steel rims. The Bill Cullen folksy charm, sharp wit, and big smile all stayed. Cullen was all over the dial, hosting Bob Stewart–created shows. In addition to his rock-solid hosting ability, Cullen was a regular panelist on *To Tell the Truth* and made guest appearances on countless other shows in the seventies.

As the seventies came to an end, Cullen was as popular as ever. He would host five other game shows during the eighties. One of these shows, *Blockbusters,* would be co-created by co-author Steve Ryan for Goodson and Todman Productions. Steve was extremely proud when Bill Cullen was nominated for his second (of three) Emmy awards for Best Game Show Emcee.

Bill Cullen was featured on his seventh and last national *TV Guide* cover on January 21, 1984, along with other game show greats Bob Barker, Jack Barry, Monty Hall, Wink Martindale, and newcomer Pat Sajak.

We miss his wit, sense of humor, and unique charm on the small screen. Please turn to list number 36 for a remarkable testimonial by his peers. I am proud to say that Bill Cullen was my friend and without his influence I would not be enjoying a successful career in TV game shows. I would like to thank Ann Cullen for bestowing me with the Bill Cullen archive of photos, kinescopes, tapes, press clippings, awards, and much, much more.

Bill Cullen: You will never be forgotten. I have very special plans for our extraordinary archive that has been entrusted to me.

Fred Wostbrock

Introduction

Take a stroll down memory lane with this nostalgic look at one of America's favorite pastimes ... the game show. Think of this book as a long, pleasurable walk through an exhilarating picturesque park. Each step you take or page you turn brings an unexpected delight or remembrance.

This fun-filled journey includes many of your favorite shows along with some of the more obscure game shows that you may or may not remember ... from the fabulous *The Price Is Right* with Barker and his Beauties to the wacky side of game show fun with *The $1.98 Beauty Show* where comic Sandra Bernhard competed for the tacky crown made of carrots and the grand prize of $1.98. You'll see the various hit shows of icon Bill Cullen and a short-lived show Bill hosted in 1979 titled *The Love Experts* featuring newcomer David Letterman as an expert panelist on how to enhance your love life (who knew?).

This book covers seven decades of a genre that has brought us terrific think tests, memory mayhem, sloppy stunts, celebrated celebrities, handsome hosts, gigantic jackpots, shocking scandals, and much, much more. Without a doubt, *The Ultimate TV Game Show Book* covers the spectrum of these exciting formats at their best and occasionally, at their worst. Whatever thie case, game shows continue to draw us to the small screen with a chance to interact and compare our knowledge and skills with the many winners and losers whom game shows have given fifteen minutes of fame. Game shows since the dawn of radio and television and now into the twenty-first century have been a part of our way of life. The fun is contagious and memorable.

Please read the acknowledgments because these special people—many of whom are personal friends—are the real stars of this book. Without their unique talents for hosting, announcing, creating new ideas, producing, writing, and designing brilliant new sets, there wouldn't be any game shows. These few hundred or so people who work in the game show industry are indeed a special breed, and we as authors and also co-workers are proud to have chosen such a career path.

To increase your reading pleasure, many lists in the book ask you to play along in classic game show fashion by guessing, matching, and recalling many of your favorite moments. Also, to further stimulate your visual senses, we have included more than 200 rare photographs, most of which have never before been seen. So, find a comfortable chair, butter the popcorn, and enjoy this one-of-a-kind look at our favorite TV pastime. We know you'll take pleasure from this nostalgic stroll. *And, that's our final answer.*

Steve Ryan and Fred Wostbrock

Twenty Ways to Construct a Hit Game Show

1. "You need to start with a strong solid idea."—Wink Martindale

2. "Find a perfect host that gels to perfection with the show." —Merv Griffin

3. "Get a good host … like me!"—Gene Rayburn

4. "A carefully crafted game show is a work of art, simple to explain, easy to follow, suspenseful to play."—Mark Goodson

5. "Create a game that everyone can enjoy."—Bill Cullen

6. "You must have an interesting concept that an audience can easily follow and be part of."—Merv Griffin

7. "The best television games, in my opinion, are based on the human experience—guessing prices on *The Price Is Right*, solving a word puzzle on *Wheel of Fortune* and *Concentration*, trying to guess a contestant's occupation on *What's My Line?* and so on." —Mark Goodson

8. "Get Bill Cullen to host your show!"—Bob Stewart

9. "Create a game that America, as well as the contestants, can have fun with."—Bob Eubanks

10. "Be creative and try to tap into the pop culture at the time." —Chuck Barris

11. "If you are going to have celebrities on your game show, try and have a mixture of talent. On *Hollywood Squares*, we had our regulars, semi-regulars, and new talents."
—Peter Marshall

12. "If you are doing a comedy game show show, such as I did with *Letters to Laugh-In* and *The Gong Show*, always be aware of making the contestant feel like the star of the show. Always add the human touch with contestants."—Gary Owens

13. "A rock solid format that's flawless will always add to the success of any game or quiz show."—Tom Kennedy

14. "The chance of winning a huge cash jackpot."—Dan Enright

15. "A format that keeps the contestants always wondering what's in the box or behind a curtain. The pure excitement of deciding what to do."—Monty Hall

16. "Combining successful elements such as tension, skill, and luck in your game, as well as a guaranteed opportunity of a prize or cash jackpot."—Merrill Heatter

17. "Get Bill Cullen to host any show."—Gene Rayburn

18. "Try to make the game as exciting as possible, as I did with all the versions of *Pyramid*."—Bob Stewart

19. "Try to create a beautiful, functional set that enhances the elements of the game and one that is pleasing for the TV audience."
—Ed Flesh (The ultimate set designer who has created works of art in game show set design, a true pioneer in his genre.)

20. "Hire Bill Cullen."—Garry Moore

Did you know ... in 1985 Wink Martindale created *Headline Chasers* with his wife, Sandy, in the kitchen of their Malibu home, while reading the *LA Times*? Wink was reading the paper and the idea for a game show featuring headlines was created. *Headline Chasers* was to become the first game show (of several) that Wink would create, and also emcee.

Without a doubt, Chuck Barris had a unique gift for tapping into the pop culture of America.

Eight of Television's
SEXIEST
Game Shows

1. ***The Amateur's Guide to Love*** (1972). Contestants were faced with matters of sex, marriage, and love.

2. ***Bedroom Buddies*** (1992). Couples had to prove how well they knew the person they were sleeping with.

3. ***Dueling for Playmates*** (1983). Male contestants vied to win a date with a Playboy Playmate.

4. ***Everything Goes*** (1981). In this strip-tease format, players undressed each other when a wrong answer was given.

5. ***The Love Experts*** (1978). A panel of four celebrities gave advice on the matters of love and romance to contestants.

6. ***Love Me, Love Me Not*** (1986). In this titillating true-false game, the object was to catch the most members of the opposite sex.

7. ***Playboy's Love and Sex Test*** (1992). A team of male players competed against a team of female players to see who knew more about sex.

8. ***Studs*** (1998). Here we found out how much men knew about women they had previously dated.

Jo Anne Worley, Geoff Edwards, and Elaine Joyce chuckle as host Bill Cullen gives his fatherly advice to a love-troubled contestant on *The Love Experts*. Soupy reminisces how his girlfriend couldn't bake an apple pie but she sure could make a banana cream.

HEARTBURN? No, it's Rayburn! Gene Rayburn is clutching the region where he fancies his heart lies to indicate he has "love" on his mind—*The Amateur's Guide to Love*, that is.

... And Eight that Sounded Sexy but Never Intended to Be So

1. *The Better Sex*
2. *The Big Surprise*
3. *Body Language*
4. *For Love or Money*
5. *Funny Boners*
6. *Let's Play Post Office*
7. *Lip Service*
8. *Lucky Partners*

Have we got your attention yet? This show hosted by Bill Anderson and Sarah Purcell was very short lived. Maybe because it had nothing to do with sex.

Did you know ... host Don Morrow was the voice of the Shell Answer Man in Shell's commercials for eighteen years?

Twenty-five Celebrities Who Looked for Love on *The Dating Game*

1. Dick Clark
2. Richard Dawson
3. Phyllis Diller
4. Farrah Fawcett
5. Sally Field
6. Cuba Gooding, Jr.
7. Mark Harmon
8. Ron Howard
9. Michael Jackson
10. Don Johnson
11. Andy Kaufman
12. Lassie
13. Paul Lynde
14. Moms Mabley
15. Lee Majors
16. Marquis Chimps
17. Steve Martin
18. Groucho Marx
19. Burt Reynolds
20. Don Rickles
21. Bob Saget
22. Arnold Schwarzenegger
23. Tom Selleck
24. Suzanne Somers
25. Adam West

Paul Lynde had a gay old time looking for love on *The Dating Game*.

Fun Facts

Holy Matrimony! The very first celebrity guest who went looking for love on *The Dating Game* was Adam West. He appeared on the show in January, 1966, to promote the premiere of his upcoming show, *Batman.*

It was host Jim Lange who wore the Batman costume that night. He made his entrance swinging in on the "Batrope."

"Hello, Jim Lange this is Adam West. I'd like to be your ... very first celebrity guest looking for love on *The Dating Game*."

Ten Unlikely Career Moves to Become Game Show Host

5

1. From trial lawyer to *Guilty or Innocent*
2. From ventriloquist to *Do You Trust Your Wife?*
3. From cartoonist to *Anyone Can Win* and *What's the Story*
4. From baseball manager to *Jackpot Bowling*
5. From TV's Tarzan to *Face the Music*
6. From Olympic gold medal decathlon winner to *Star Games*
7. From TV's Maverick to *Sale of the Century*
8. From burlesque stripper to *Think Fast*
9. From Sherlock Holmes on the silver screen to *Your Lucky Clue*
10. From prime-time TV creator to *Quiz Kids*

Can you name the personalities who made the career moves?

Answers on page 249.

WOW! I wonder if these kids know that Norman Lear created such shows as *All in the Family, Good Times, The Jeffersons, Maude,* and *Mary Hartman, Mary Hartman.*

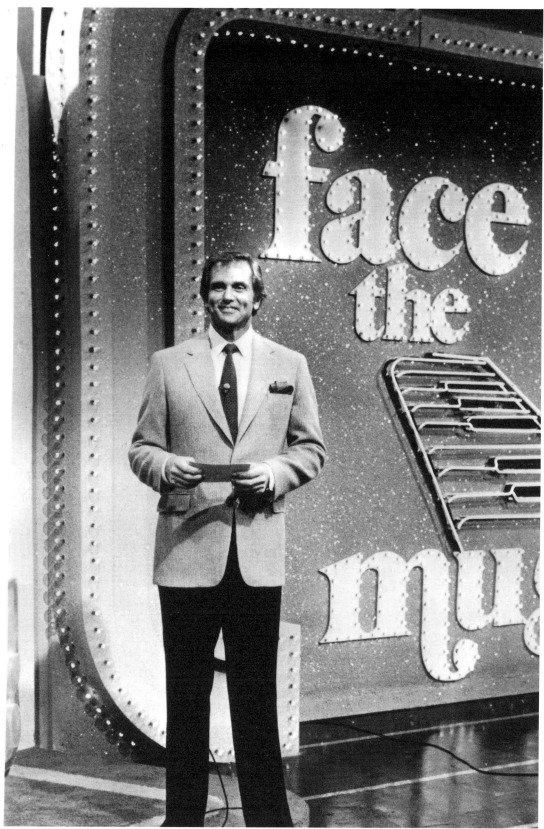

Do, Re, Mi, Fa, So, La, "T"... for Tarzan. Who would have thought it? Ron Ely did a swinging job as host of *Face the Music*.

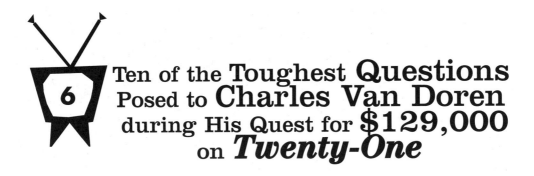

Ten of the Toughest Questions Posed to Charles Van Doren during His Quest for $129,000 on *Twenty-One*

1. Because of a disagreement with his commanding general, Ulysses Grant was virtually placed under arrest for a brief time early in 1862. Who was the commanding general of the Union Army then?

2. Grandsons of Joseph Medill, two of the most successful journalists in the country from 1914 on, were the owners and managers of the *Chicago Tribune* and the *New York Daily News*. Name them.

3. It's well known that some of Henry the Eighth's six wives fared better than others. He divorced his first wife, Katherine of Aragon. He married his sixth, Catherine Parr, just a few years before he died. Name the second, third, fourth, and fifth wives of Henry the Eighth, and describe their fates.

4. A prominent labor leader, author of *Wall and Bars,* once ran for the presidency of the United States while serving a term in jail. Who was he?

5. Militant womanhood asserted itself at a convention in Seneca Falls, New York, in 1848, when the movement for women's suffrage in the United States began. Name three of the four women who were the earliest leaders of this movement.

6. I will give you a quote from *As You Like It* —
   All the world's a stage,
   And all the men and women merely players;
   They have their exits and their entrances
   And one man in his time plays many parts,
   His acts being seven ages.
   Give me the "seven ages of man" in this speech.

7. Helen Hayes, often referred to as "the first lady of the theater," starred in a play which was based on *The Cherry Orchard*. Tell us 1. Who wrote *The Cherry Orchard?* 2. What was the name of the American version? 3. Who wrote this version? And, 4. Who directed it?

8. During Lincoln's administration, he had two vice presidents and two secretaries of war. Name them.

9. The first case brought before the UN Security Council was a complaint in January, 1946, demanding an end to Russian interference in a particular country. Tell us 1. What country brought the complaint to the UN, and 2. Who was the chief Russian delegate, and 3. Who was the chief American delegate to the UN Security Council at that time?

10. The Balearic Islands lie off the east coast of Spain, in the Mediterranean. Name the four principal Balearic Islands.

Answers on page 249.

Poor Mr. Taslenko. He hasn't got a clue that Charles Van Doren was scripted to be the winner.

... And the Oscar goes to Charles Van Doren for his best supporting actor role in the fixed prime-time game show *Twenty-One*.

Thirteen Lucky Game
Shows that Became
Casino Games

1. *Concentration*
2. *The Dating Game*
3. *Family Feud*
4. *Hollywood Squares*
5. *Jeopardy!*
6. *Let's Make a Deal*
7. *The Newlywed Game*
8. *Press Your Luck*
9. *The Price Is Right*
10. *Pyramid*
11. *Sale of the Century*
12. *To Tell the Truth*
13. *Wheel of Fortune*

Concentration has the distinction of being NBC's longest-running daytime game show. Here we see three great hosts of *Concentration*, Jack Narz, Alex Trebek, and Ed McMahon, joined by Steve Ryan, who created all of the rebuses for *Classic Concentration* and Bally's Concentration slot machine.

The wheel keeps turning, first as America's number-one game show and now as America's number-one slot machine game.

8 Two Game Shows Regis Philbin Hosted before His Big Hit, *Who Wants to Be a Millionaire*

1. *Almost Anything Goes,* ABC, July 31, 1975.
2. *The Neighbors,* ABC, December 29, 1975.

Even before *Who Wants to Be a Millionaire,* it's easy to see that Regis had a great fan base.

Here Regis is on *The Neighbors.* All of the game shows Regis Philbin ever hosted were on ABC.

Six Landmarks for Mark Goodson and Bill Todman

1948   *Winner Take All,* hosted by Bud Collyer, premieres on CBS, becoming the first Goodson-Todman show to appear on network television.

1950   *What's My Line?,* hosted by John Daly, premieres on CBS. By the time *What's My Line?* left the air in 1967, it had become the second longest running prime time show on television, second only to *The Ed Sullivan Show.*

1950s   *Beat the Clock, I've Got a Secret, The Price Is Right,* and *To Tell the Truth* all become instant hits.

1960s   *Password,* with host Allen Ludden, becomes an instant hit on CBS. *The Match Game,* with puckish host Gene Rayburn, also strikes gold on NBC.

1972   *The Price Is Right,* with its new host Bob Barker, debuts on CBS and proves to be the longest running game show in the history of television.

1976   *Family Feud* takes America by storm, as does host Richard Dawson and his kissing of contestants.

Mark Goodson presents Carol Burnett with the silver *Password All-Stars* award for best celebrity player.

Bob Barker gets a surprise visit from Mark Goodson on the set of *The Price Is Right*. Mark thanked Bob for making *The Price Is Right* number one, a record that still holds today.

10 Five Classic Shows that Began with a Title Other than the Classic We Know and Love

1. *To Tell the Truth*
2. *The Price Is Right*
3. *Wheel of Fortune*
4. *Jeopardy!*
5. *Family Feud*

Can you match the classic game show with its original title that never made it to the airwaves?

A. *Shopper's Bazaar*
B. *Nothing but the Truth*
C. *What's the Question?*
D. *Auctionaire*
E. *On a Roll*

Answers on page 249.

Who knew *Shopper's Bazaar* would evolve into TV's biggest all-time ratings winner ... *Wheel of Fortune*? But wait, where's the wheel?

... Here it is behind host Chuck Woolery. In a stroke of genius this vertical wheel became the most famous horizontal wheel in television history.

Eleven
Game Show
Firsts

1. **First regularly scheduled TV game show:**
   CBS Television Quiz for local CBS/WCBW with host Gil Fates, July 2, 1941.
2. **First network radio transition to television:**
   Missus Goes-a-Shopping for CBS with host John Reed King, August 3, 1944.
3. **First network game show:**
   Cash and Carry for the Dumont Network with host Dennis James,
   June 20, 1949.
4. **First Goodson-Todman game show:**
   Winner Take All for CBS with host Bill Cullen, July 1, 1948.
5. **First female game show host:**
   Arlene Francis on *Blind Date* on ABC, May 5, 1949.
6. **First daytime game show:**
   Remember This Date on NBC with host Bill Stern, November 16, 1950.
7. **First successful game show to team celebrities and civilians:**
   Password on CBS with host Allen Ludden, October 2, 1961.
8. **First game show to use neon lights:**
   Baffle on NBC with host Dick Enberg, March 26, 1973.
9. **First African-American game show host:**
   Adam Wade on *Musical Chairs* on CBS, June 16, 1975.
10. **First cable game show:**
    Everything Goes on the Playboy Channel with host Kip Addotta,
    September 12, 1981.
11. **First game show to utilize computer animation:**
    Catch Phrase, seen in syndication with host Art James, with animated
    puzzles by Steve Ryan, September 16, 1985.

Bonus Fact

Baffle—an updated version of 1965's syndicated game show *PDQ*—replaced *Concentration*, NBC's longest-running daytime game show.

Is the happy contestant pleased to win $5,000 and a new car ... or is she just shielding her eyes from the very bright neon?

Did you know ... host Adam Wade received a basketball scholarship to Virginia State College? In 1957, he was hired by Dr. Jonas Salk as an assistant on the polio virus research team.

12 Twenty-six Emcees Who Were Mystery Guests on *What's My Line?*

1. Steve Allen
2. Larry Blyden
3. Wally Bruner
4. Johnny Carson
5. Dick Clark
6. Bud Collyer
7. Bert Convy
8. Bill Cullen
9. John Daly
10. Richard Dawson
11. Hugh Downs
12. Art Fleming
13. Joe Garagolia
14. Monty Hall
15. Robert Q. Lewis
16. Art Linkletter
17. Allen Ludden
18. Hal March
19. Peter Marshall
20. Groucho Marx
21. Ed McMahon
22. Garry Moore
23. Jack Narz
24. Jack Paar
25. Bert Parks
26. Gene Rayburn

Likeable, loveable Bill was a great host, a great panelist, and a fabulous mystery guest.

The 876th and final network show aired on September 3, 1967. John Daly, who had always been the emergency mystery guest, finally got his chance to be the mystery guest. *What's My Line?* won the Emmy awards for Best Quiz or Audience Participation Show three times, in 1952, 1953, and 1958.

Fifteen Shows that Were Reborn with New Titles

1. *Pantomine Quiz* (1950) ... *Stump the Stars* (1962) ... *Celebrity Charades* (1979)

2. *Who's the Boss?* (1954) ... *Who Pays?* (1959)

3. *Do You Trust Your Wife?* (1956) ... *Who Do You Trust?* (1958)

4. *Concentration* (1958) ... *Classic Concentration* (1987)

5. *College Bowl* (1959) ... *Campus All-Star Challenge* (1990)

6. *Password* (1961) ... *Password Plus* (1979) ... *Super Password* (1984)

7. *What's This Song?* (1964) ... *Win with the Stars* (1968)

8. *PDQ* (1965) ... *Baffle* (1973)

9. *I'll Bet* (1965) ... *It's Your Bet* (1969)

10. *Oh My Word* (1966) ... *Take My Word for It* (1982)

11. *Everybody's Talking* (1967) ... *Hollywood's Talking* (1973)

12. *Pay Cards!* (1968) ... *Super Pay Cards!* (1981)

13. *He Said, She Said* (1967) ... *Tattletales* (1974)

14. *All about Faces* (1971) ... *Anything for Money* (1984)

15. *Second Chance* (1977) ... *Press Your Luck* (1983)

Fun Fact

Jim Peck was under contract to the ABC network and *Second Chance* was the third game show that he emceed for ABC. His first show was *Big Showdown* in 1974 and his second was *Hot Seat* in 1976.

Exit the devil and Jim Peck. Enter Peter Tomarken and the Whammy.

Six Game Show Hosts Who Said "Goodbye" on Friday and "Hello" on Monday with Different Game Shows on the Same Network

1. Bill Cullen, *Three on a Match* to *Winning Streak*
2. Art James, *Blank Check* to *Magnificent Marble Machine*
3. Tom Kennedy, *50 Grand Slam* to *Name That Tune*
4. Jim Lange, *Spin-Off* to *Give-n-Take*
5. Allen Ludden, *Password All-Stars* to *Password*
6. Alex Trebek, *Wizard of Odds* to *High Rollers*

In one weekend Art James went from TV's biggest check to TV's biggest pinball machine.

Fun Fact

The giant pinball set took over sixty days to build. The machine contained 250 pounds of nails, four miles of wiring, thirty-eight gallons of glue, twenty-three coiled springs, enough glass for ten car windshields, twenty-five two-pound balls, and fourteen gallons of gold paint for the pinballs used.

15 Eight Popular Songs that Became Game Show Theme Songs

1. "A Pretty Girl Is Like a Melody"
2. "Spanish Flea"
3. "We're in the Money"
4. "Ain't She Sweet"
5. "A Swingin' Safari"
6. "Book of Love"
7. "Everything's Coming up Roses"
8. "Three Blind Mice"

Can you match the game show with the popular song?

A. *The Match Game*
B. *Seven Keys*
C. *The $1.98 Beauty Show*
D. *The Big Payoff*
E. *Your First Impression*
F. *The Newlywed Game* (1988 only)
G. *Doctor I.Q.*
H. *The Dating Game*

Answers on page 250.

It's a tough job, but somebody had to do it. As you can see, Rip Taylor had his hands full hosting *The $1.98 Beauty Show.*

Fun Fact
Female comic Sandra Bernhard was a contestant on *The $1.98 Beauty Show* in 1978.

BRADFORD DILLMAN   STEVE McQUEEN   DANE CLARK

Were you watching when Richard M. Nixon, then running for governor of California, made an appearance in 1962, or when actors Charles Bronson, Buster Keaton, and Rod Serling guested in 1963? Johnny Carson made a rare appearance in 1962.

Ten Real Names of Classic Game Show Hosts ...

 1. Bud Collyer = Clayton Heermance, Jr.
 2. Richard Dawson = Colin Emm
 3. Monty Hall = Maurice Halprin
 4. Dennis James = Demie Sposa
 5. Tom Kennedy = Jim Narz
 6. Allen Ludden = Allen Ellsworth
 7. Peter Marshall = Pierre La Cock
 8. Wink Martindale = Winston Martindale
 9. Garry Moore = Thomas Morfit
10. Gene Rayburn = Eugene Rubessa

... And One Adorable Letter Turner

 1. Vanna White = Vanna Rosich

Tom Kennedy meet Jack Narz. No. Jack Narz meet Jim Kennedy. No. Tom Narz meet Jack Narz. No. Ahhhh, forget it. That's the brother of Jack Narz, Jim Narz who changed his name to Tom Kennedy.

Fun Fact
Monty Hall was named Humanitarian of the Year by Variety Club. He received other top honors from around the country and the world for his generous charity work.

Four Game Shows
that Featured Puzzles
Created by Steve Ryan

1. *Body Language*
2. *Catch Phrase*
3. *Classic Concentration*
4. *Password Plus*

Here we see … Carol Burnett, Alan Ludden, and Vicki Lawrence playing *Alphabetics*. Mark Goodson was a big fan of Carol Burnett's (she loved to play *Password*) and often utilized her talent. In an office run-through in preparation for the return of the new and improved *Password '79* (as the show was to be titled), Carol made the comment, "This is more than 'Password,' it's 'Password Plus.'" Mark Goodson recognized the elegance and genius of Carol's remark and gave the show a brand new name … *Password Plus!*

Steve poses with one of his *Classic Concentration* rebus puzzles. Can you solve it? That's right! ST + EVE, R + EYE + YAWN = STEVE RYAN.

Three Shocking Moments in Game Show History

1. Charles Van Doren admits to cheating on *Twenty-One*. *Twenty-One* was featured in the 1994 motion picture *Quiz Show*, which dramatized the late 1950s Congressional investigation into the rigging of *Twenty-One*.

2. One crafty contestant beats the system and wins a bundle on *Press Your Luck*. It wasn't cheating, but the producers wasted no time reformatting the game board so that the house could never be flimflammed again.

3. In an outrageous moment of spontaneous combustion Jaye P. Morgan bares her bosom on *The Gong Show*. It caught Chuck Barris, the censors, and the lucky studio audience totally off guard. Too bad it wasn't in the days of live television. Home viewers had to settle for the censored version.

Not to be upstaged by Jaye P. Morgan, Jamie Farr decides to get into the act.

It was great TV back in 1957 but the #*@% would hit the fan in 1958.

Three Landmarks for Bob Stewart Productions

1966   ***Eye Guess*** with host Bill Cullen is the first show to premiere from Bob Stewart after his long association with Goodson-Todman Productions.

1973   ***Three on a Match*** with host Bill Cullen debuts on NBC.

1974   ***The $10,000 Pyramid,*** with original host Dick Clark, begins its impressive run. The show would grow through five title changes to eventually become ***The $100,000 Pyramid*** in 1985.

Bob Stewart and his meticulous eye for perfection received sixteen Emmy nominations for Outstanding Game Show and won the award nine times for *Pyramid*.

Bob Stewart was such a huge fan of Bill Cullen's that he asked Cullen to host eight of his game show creations. Here's Bill from 1971 on *Three on a Match*.

Nine Different Hosts of *To Tell the Truth*

1. **Bud Collyer**
2. **Garry Moore**
3. **Joe Garagolia**
4. **Robin Ward**
5. **Gordon Elliott**
6. **Alex Trebek**
7. **Lynn Swann**
8. **John O'Hurley**
9. **Mike Wallace**

Can you identify which host made the pilot for *To Tell the Truth* back in 1956 but was not picked up as the host of the show for air?

Answer on page 250.

Garry Moore and his cast of panelists were magical. Who could ever forget Bill Cullen, Peggy Cass, and Kitty Carlisle?

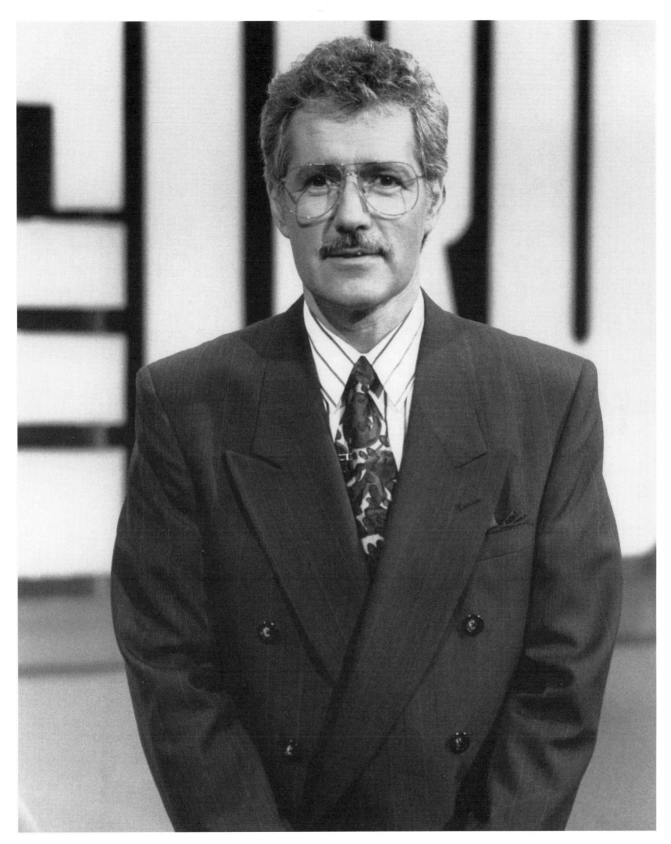

Fun Fact
Alex Trebek also hosted the program preceding
To Tell the Truth on NBC, *Classic Concentration,* giving him a full hour on daytime television.

Ten Questions that Made Couples Blush on *The Newlywed Game*

1. How does your wife lick her ice cream cone? Up and down or around in a circle?

2. How many times on an average does your husband "masticate?"

3. Which one of these hamburger slogans will your partner say best describes your first night together: "Have it your way," "You deserve a break, today," or "Where's the beef?"

4. In the delicatessen of love, how will your partner say you think he behaved last night: Like a hot pastrami, like a cold turkey, like a deviled egg, or like chopped liver?

5. Which one of the following will your partner say you think best describes his behavior lately in the romance department: Unconcerned, unconventional, uncoordinated, or unconscious?

6. While you sleep, will your partner say that the two of you are more often: Toe to toe, cheek to cheek, back to back, or nose to nose?

7. Last night, in the whoopie department, will your partner say that you behaved more like: An Odd-vark, a ham-ster, a praying Mantis, or a draggin' fly?

8. The very first time you and your partner spent the night together, will he say you think he behaved more like: Rambo, Columbo, or Dumbo?

9. Lately, in the romance department, will your partner say you've been behaving more like: A second-hand man, a minute-man, or a long-shoreman?

10. Where was the most unusual place you ever made whoopie?

Fun Fact
Probably the most unexpected and embarrassing answer ever given on *The Newlywed Game* was in response to question number 10, when one member of a team responded with "In the butt, Bob."

Are you serious? You mean to tell me your husband actually masticates three times a week.

You nit wit, I lick my ice cream cones up and down not around in a circle.

Three Game Shows that Called the Ed Sullivan Theater Home

1. *The $10,000 Pyramid*
2. *Pass the Buck*
3. *What's My Line?*

Fred Wostbrock first met the man who would most influence his game show career in 1978. That great man was Bill Cullen, here hosting the Bob Stewart creation *Pass the Buck*. Over the years Fred and Bill would become great friends.

56

Three Game Shows that Called the Ed Sullivan Theater Home

1. *The $10,000 Pyramid*
2. *Pass the Buck*
3. *What's My Line?*

Fred Wostbrock first met the man who would most influence his game show career in 1978. That great man was Bill Cullen, here hosting the Bob Stewart creation *Pass the Buck*. Over the years Fred and Bill would become great friends.

56

After a long, careful search, Wally Bruner was selected by *What's My Line?* producers Bill Todman and Mark Goodson to carry on the torch.

Fifteen Emcees Who Hosted the Same Game Shows during Different Runs

1. Jack Berry, *The Joker's Wild*
2. Dick Clark, *Pyramids*
3. Bert Convy, *Tattletales*
4. Richard Dawson, *Family Feud*
5. Bob Eubanks, *The Newlywed Game*
6. Art Fleming, *Jeopardy!*
7. Monty Hall, *Let's Make a Deal*
8. Tom Kennedy, *You Don't Say!* and *Name That Tune*
9. Jim Lange, *The Dating Game*
10. Allen Ludden, *Password*
11. Wink Martindale, *Gambit* and *Tic Tac Dough*
12. Gene Rayburn, *Match Game*
13. David Ruprecht, *Supermarket Sweep*
14. Alex Trebek, *High Rollers* and *Battlestars*
15. Chuck Woolery, *Scrabble*

1963 ... the wet look.

1975 ... the dry look.

Nine Shows with the Shortest Titles

1. *Go*
2. *Vs.*
3. *Why?*
4. *Jep!*
5. *E.S.P.*
6. *Whew*
7. *Bzzz!*
8. *Cram*
9. *Debt*

Here's K.O. hosting G-O ... Kevin O'Connell was a local weatherman at KNBC before hosting Go.

Multi-millionaire Wink Martindale finds himself in *Debt* in 1996.

25 Eleven Funny Men Who Have Stars on the Hollywood Walk of Fame Who Also Hosted Game Shows

1. Steve Allen
2. Milton Berle
3. Johnny Carson
4. Bill Cosby
5. Jackie Gleason
6. Ernie Kovacs
7. Groucho Marx
8. Gary Owens
9. Carl Reiner
10. Rip Taylor
11. Dick Van Dyke

Can you match these funny men with the game shows they hosted?
(Two hosted the same show.)

A. *You Bet Your Life*
B. *Earn Your Vacation*
C. *Jackpot Bowling*
D. *Celebrity Game*
E. *I've Got a Secret*
F. *The $1.98 Beauty Show*
G. *You're in the Picture*
H. *Gamble on Love*
I. *Laugh Line*
J. *The Gong Show*

Answers on page 250.

Funny man Jackie Gleason decided *You're in the Picture* was no laughing matter and cancelled his own show after only one airing.

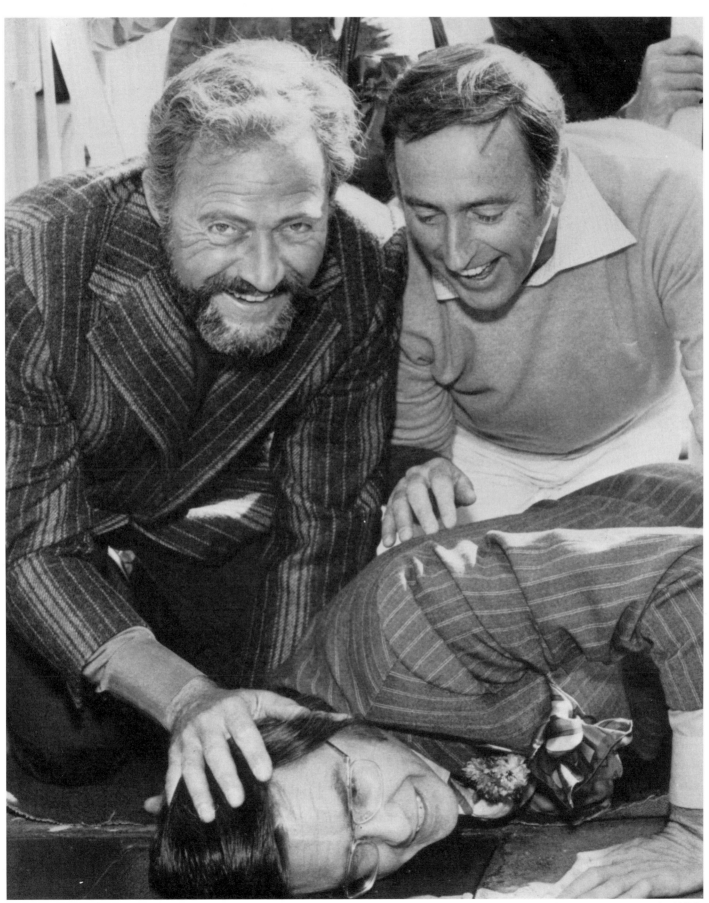

Not only does Gary Owens have his star on the Hollywood Walk of Fame but he also has his ear in cement at NBC.

Twenty-six Game Shows on the Air in a Single Season

1. *The Big Showdown*
2. *Celebrity Sweepstakes*
3. *Concentration*
4. *Cross-Wits*
5. *The Diamond Head Game*
6. *Gambit*
7. *High Rollers*
8. *Hollywood Squares*
9. *Jackpot*
10. *Jeopardy!*
11. *The Joker's Wild*
12. *Let's Make a Deal*
13. *Liar's Club*
14. *Match Game '75*
15. *Money Maze*
16. *Name That Tune*
17. *Now You See It*
18. *Password All-Stars*
19. *The Price Is Right*
20. *Split Second*
21. *Tattletales*
22. *The $10,000 Pyramid*
23. *To Tell the Truth*
24. *Treasure Hunt*
25. *What's My Line?*
26. *Winning Streak*

Fun Fact
That's a record number of game shows on the air at the same time, and the year was 1975.

If you were good at solving riddles, *Jackpot*, hosted by Geoff Edwards, was your kind of show.

Money Maze host Nick Clooney is the father of movie star George Clooney.

Twenty-nine Emcee Birth Places

1. Bob Barker = Darringtron, Washington
2. Chuck Barris = Philadelphia, Pennsylvania
3. Tom Bergeron = Havenhill, Massachusetts
4. Brooke Burns = Dallas, Texas
5. Dick Clark = Mt. Vernon, New York
6. Bill Cullen = Pittsburgh, Pennsylvania
7. Richard Dawson = Gagport, England
8. Geoff Edwards = Westfield, New Jersey
9. Bob Eubanks = Flint, Michigan
10. Monty Hall = Winnipeg, Canada
11. Tom Kennedy = Louisville, Kentucky
12. Jim Lange = St. Paul, Minnesota
13. Allen Ludden = Mineral Point, Wisconsin
14. Peter Marshall = Huntington, West Virginia
15. Wink Martindale = Jackson, Tennessee
16. Garry Moore = Baltimore, Maryland
17. Todd Newton = St. Louis, Missouri
18. Gary Owens = Mitchell, South Dakota
19. Regis Philbin = New York, New York
20. Jeff Probst = Wichita, Kansas
21. Gene Rayburn = Christopher, Illinois
22. Joe Rogan = Newark, New Jersey
23. David Ruprecht = St. Louis, Missouri
24. Ryan Seacrest = Atlanta, Georgia
25. Marc Summers = Indianapolis, Indiana
26. Alex Trebek = Sudbury, Ontario
27. Mark L. Walberg = Florence, South Carolina
28. Vanna White = Conway, South Carolina
29. Chuck Woolery = Ashland, Kentucky

"Are the producers trying to tell me something? Do I still have a job? Are you sending me home to Pittsburgh?"

The password is "Mineral Point." That's Allen Ludden's hometown.

Two Shows where Animals Relieved Themselves on Live TV

(when you gotta go, you gotta go!)

1. *The Price Is Right* (elephants)
2. *I've Got a Secret* (cow)

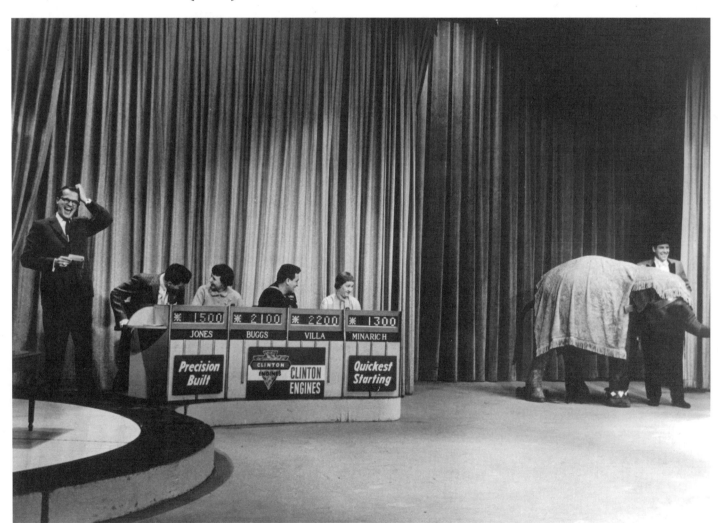

Going, going ...

Fun Fact
Bill Cullen was an eyewitness to both moments. He was hosting *The Price Is Right* and a panelist on *I've Got a Secret*.

… Gone.

Four Landmarks for Merrill Heatter and Bob Quigley Productions

1960   The first Heatter-Quigley game show, *Video Village,* debuts with Jack Narz as host on CBS.

1966   The classic *Hollywood Squares,* with host Peter Marshall, debuts on NBC and runs successfully into the 1980s.

1972   *Gambit,* with host Wink Martindale, debuts on CBS.

1973   *High Rollers,* with host Alex Trebek, debuts on NBC.

Merrill Heatter and Bob Quigley proved to be a dynamic duo creating dozens of shows together. Here they celebrate ten years of *Hollywood Squares.*

A dapper Jack Narz and the beautiful Joanne Copeland prepare to tumble the chuck-a-luck on *Video Village.*

Six Trivia Quiz Answers that All Begin with the Letter "W"

1. What was the last name of the host that Pat Sajak replaced on *Wheel of Fortune* in 1981?

2. Arlene Francis, Dorothy Kilgallen, and Bennett Cerf were all regular panelists on what CBS Sunday night game show?

3. Prior to *The Tonight Show,* what daytime game show did Johnny Carson host with Ed McMahon as his sidekick?

4. On what show would you hear the classic question, "Is it bigger than a bread box?"

5. Give the last name of the television newsman who replaced Jack Barry as host of *The Big Surprise.*

6. What was the first Goodson-Todman game show to be broadcast on network television?

Answers on page 250.

The King of Late-Night Television, Johnny Carson, and his sidekick, Ed McMahon, were inseparable for five decades. They even hung out together in the make-up room.

Long before *60 Minutes,* here we see Mike Wallace hosting *The Big Surprise* with guest celebrity contestant Errol Flynn.

31 Twenty-two Game Shows from One Director
(a record achievement by Jerome Shaw)

1. *All Star Blitz*
2. *The Amateur's Guide to Love*
3. *Baffle*
4. *Bargain Hunters*
5. *Battlestars*
6. *Double Exposure*
7. *Gambit*
8. *High Rollers*
9. *Hollywood Squares*
10. *Hot Seat*
11. *I'm Telling*
12. *Keep Talking*
13. *The Magnificent Marble Machine*
14. *Name Droppers*
15. *100 Grand*
16. *$1,000,000 Chance of a Lifetime*
17. *PDQ*
18. *Runaround*
19. *Sale of the Century*
20. *Storybook Squares*
21. *To Say the Least*
22. *Video Village*

That's Tom Kennedy hosting his first Heatter-Quigley game show, *To Say the Least.*

Jim Peck says the pressure is on when you're in the *Hot Seat,* but the reward is worth the heat.

Twelve Classic Game Show Hosts Who Stand Six Feet Tall or Taller

1. Art Fleming, 6'4"
2. Peter Marshall, 6'3"
3. Jim Lange, 6'2"
4. Wink Martindale, 6'2"
5. Chuck Woolery, 6'2"
6. Bob Barker, 6'1"
7. Bob Eubanks, 6'1"
8. Tom Kennedy, 6'1"
9. Gary Owens, 6'1"
10. Geoff Edwards, 6'1"
11. Monty Hall, 6'
12. Allen Ludden, 6'

Tom Kennedy is pleased to shake hands with fellow game show hosts and members of the "tall club."

Answer: A giant of a man with talent to match. Question: Who is Art Fleming?

33

Five Versions of *Pyramid* Hosted by Dick Clark

1. *The $10,000 Pyramid*
2. *The $20,000 Pyramid*
3. *The $25,000 Pyramid*
4. *The $50,000 Pyramid*
5. *The $100,000 Pyramid*

This $25,000 win took Penny Marshall's breath away.

Two ageless classics: Dick Clark and the *Pyramid*.

Six Shared Birthdays

1. January 8—Bob Eubanks and Elvis Presley
2. February 18—Bill Cullen and Vanna White
3. February 26—Joe Garagolia and Tom Kennedy
4. August 25—Monty Hall and Regis Philbin
5. November 11—Marc Summers and Stubby Kaye
6. November 20—Richard Dawson and Jack Linkletter

Birthday boy, Bill Cullen is happy to share his special day with Vanna White.

Party animal Tom Kennedy is happy to send his birthday wishes to Joe Garagolia.

35 Seven Game Shows with Popular Icons

1. Barker's Beauties
2. Dr. Reason A. Goodwin
3. Whammy
4. The Town Crier
5. Kenny the Cop
6. Beulah the Buzzer
7. Edgar the Talking Jukebox

We name the icons, you name the shows.

Answers on page 250.

Bob says come on down to his Barker's Beauties. That's Janice Pennington and Anitra Ford.

Town Crier Kenny Williams pulls over Mayor Monty and gives him a warning about speeding in the village. That's Eileen Barton riding shotgun.

36 Thirteen Game Show Hosts Who Consider Bill Cullen the Best Game Show Host Ever

1. Dick Clark
2. Bob Eubanks
3. Monty Hall
4. Tom Kennedy
5. Art Linkletter
6. Allen Ludden
7. Peter Marshall
8. Wink Martindale
9. Ed McMahon
10. Garry Moore
11. Jack Narz
12. Gary Owens
13. Regis Philbin

Bill Cullen often guest-starred on Dick's *$10,000 Pyramid* and *$20,000 Pyramid,* and Dick Clark, in turn was a guest on Bill's *$25,000 Pyramid.*

Wink says Bill is the best host ever, and Bill returns the compliment.

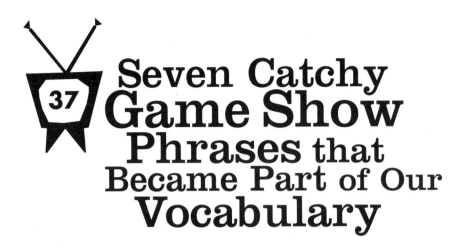

37 Seven Catchy Game Show Phrases that Became Part of Our Vocabulary

1. "Come on down!" *(The Price Is Right)*
2. "Enter and sign in please!" *(What's My Line?)*
3. "I'd like to buy a vowel." *(Wheel of Fortune)*
4. "Is it bigger than a breadbox?" *(What's My Line?)*
5. "Say the secret word." *(You Bet Your Life)*
6. "Will the real (John Doe) please stand up!" *(To Tell the Truth)*
7. "Is that your final answer?" *(Who Wants to Be a Millionaire)*

The pulse-pounding *Who Wants to Be a Millionaire* single-handedly revived the prime-time game show genre in 1999.

Vanna adds just the right amount of sex appeal to make buying a vowel exciting.

Five Game Shows that Bob Goen Hosted before *Entertainment Tonight*

1. *Blackout*
2. *Born Lucky*
3. *Hollywood Game*
4. *Home Shopping Game*
5. *Perfect Match*
6. *Wheel of Fortune*

Newcomer Bob Goen hosting his first game show, *Perfect Match.* He kept on Goen all the way to *Entertainment Tonight.*

On July 17, 1989 Bob Goen became the last daytime host of *Wheel of Fortune*.

39
Two Landmarks for Monty Hall and Stefan Hatos Productions

1963   ***Let's Make a Deal,*** with Monty Hall, debuts on NBC. The enormous popularity of Monty and the show assures that ***Let's Make a Deal*** will appear in numerous markets throughout the '60s, '70s, '80s, and '90s and into the twenty-first century.

1972   ***Split Second,*** with host Tom Kennedy, debuts on ABC.

Creator Monty Hall congratulates Tom Kennedy on his rapid-fire hosting abilities on *Split Second.*

Fun Fact

In the fourteen-year run of *Let's Make a Deal* as a network show, it broke all records for game show popularity with Monty Hall as host. When *Let's Make a Deal* left the NBC daytime schedule to move to the ABC (December 30, 1968) daytime schedule, NBC soon lost millions in daytime advertising revenue and ABC became the number-one daytime network. Here, Stefan Hatos and Monty Hall kick back and savor the success of *Let's Make a Deal.*

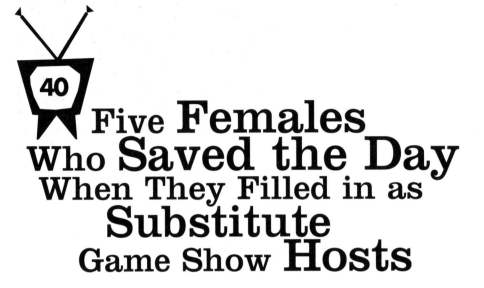

Five Females Who Saved the Day When They Filled in as Substitute Game Show Hosts

1. Arlene Francis
2. Celeste Holm
3. Ginger Rogers
4. Sally Struthers
5. Betty White

Can you match the game show with the substitute host?
(Two substituted for the same show.)

A. *The Price Is Right*
B. *Password*
C. *The $64,000 Question*
D. *Win, Lose or Draw*

Answers on page 251.

The darling of game shows—Miss Arlene Francis.   She began her career co-starring with Bela Lugosi in the movie *Murders in the Rue Morgue.*

Allen Ludden met Betty White during a 1962 summer stock production of *Critic's Choice*. They enjoyed playing husband and wife on stage and soon followed suit in real life.

41

Two (and Only Two) Game Shows Debuted in 1970, and Wink Martindale Hosted Them Both

1. *Can You Top This?,* syndicated, January 26, 1970.
2. *Words and Music,* NBC, September 28, 1970.

Wink Martindale and Dick Gauiter laugh at Danny Thomas's 1970 humor.

Wink Martindale smiles even though *Words and Music* was short-lived. His mega-hit, *Gambit*, was soon to follow.

Nineteen Game Show Hosts Who Were Guests on Peter Marshall's Classic *Hollywood Squares*

1. Dick Clark
2. Bob Clayton
3. Hugh Downs
4. Bob Eubanks
5. Art Fleming
6. Joe Garagolia
7. Monty Hall
8. Art James
9. Dennis James
10. Tom Kennedy
11. Art Linkletter
12. Lohman and Barkley
13. Wink Martindale
14. Jim McKrell
15. Garry Moore
16. Jack Narz
17. Gene Rayburn
18. Alex Trebek
19. Chuck Woolery

The all-stars of the NBC line-up: Bob Clayton, Peter Marshall, Art Fleming, and Art James.

Fun Fact

Peter Marshall was not the original host for *Hollywood Squares*. When the pilot was taped for CBS, veteran game show host Bert Parks was seen as the Master of the *Hollywood Squares*. When NBC picked up the show, they chose Marshall, who had started his career at age fourteen as NBC's youngest page and was also part of a comedy team with Tommy Noonan. Peter Marshall won five Emmys for his emceeing style, and creators/executive producers Merrill Heatter and Bob Quigley won four Emmys. Peter won two Emmys in 1974, one for Best Host in a Game Show and the other for Daytime Host of the Year. Here, the Master of the *Hollywood Squares:* Peter Marshall. Rose Marie, along with Paul Lynde, was a regular on *Hollywood Squares,* on both the daytime and syndicated versions. The legendary Rose Marie was the Arlene Francis of the West Coast.

Five Bald Game Show Hosts

1. Joe Garagolia
2. Carl Reiner
3. Al Roker
4. Paul Shafer
5. Ahmed Zappa

Bonus Fact

Carl Reiner was the only host to appear with and without hair.

Hair today ...

... Gone tomorrow.

Six Game Shows Hosted by Ventriloquists and Their Dummies

1. *Celebrity Charades* with ventriloquist Jay Johnson and Squeaky (1979).

2. *Come Closer* with ventriloquist Jimmy Nelson & Danny O'Day, Humphrey Higby and Farfel the Dog (1954).

3. *Funny Boners* with ventriloquist Jimmy Weldon and Webster Webfoot (1954).

4. *Do You Trust Your Wife?* with ventriloquist Edgar Bergen and Charlie McCarthy, Mortimer Snerd and Effie Klinker (1956).

5. *Runaround* with ventriloquist Paul Winchell and Jerry Mahoney and Knucklehead Smiff (1972).

6. *What's My Name?* with ventriloquist Paul Winchell and Jerry Mahoney and Knucklehead Smiff (1950).

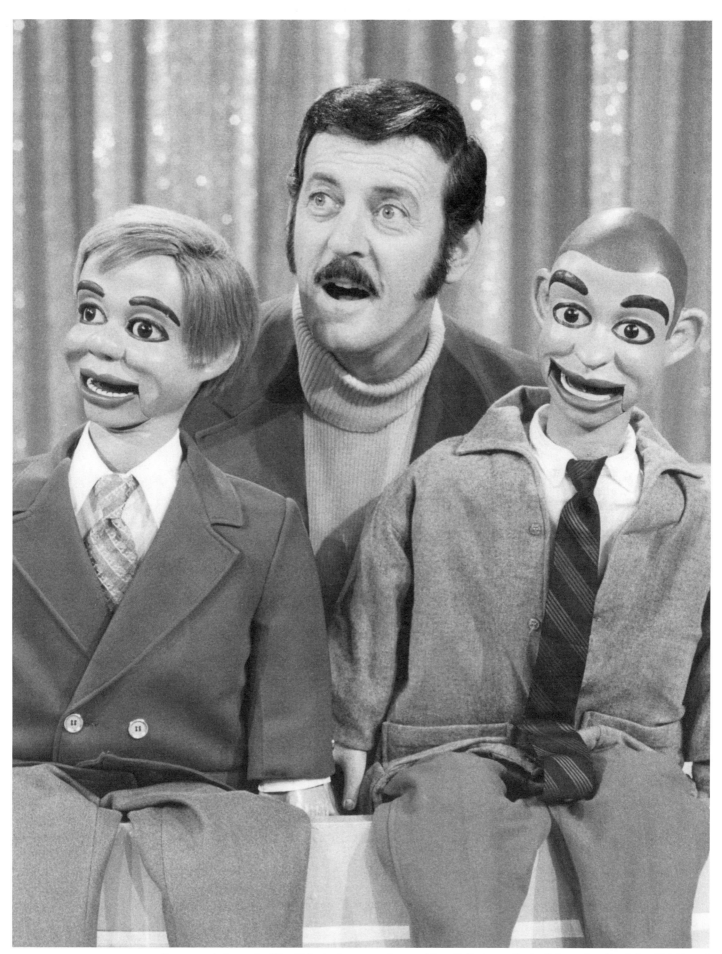

Few people know that Paul Winchell was no dummy himself. He is credited with inventing the first artificial heart.

Squeaky says to Jay, "Would you like me to turn my head and cough now?"

Seven Good Guys Who Appeared on Game Shows

1. Johnny Carson
2. Leonardo DiCaprio
3. Clint Eastwood
4. Cuba Gooding, Jr.
5. Phil Hartman
6. Greg Kinnear
7. Jerry Seinfeld

Can you match up these celebrities with the game shows they appeared on?

A. This star, who later went on to late-night talk show fame, started out in show business hosting a 1954 game show called *Earn Your Vacation.*

B. This Oscar-winning actor was looking for love in all the right places as a contestant on *The Dating Game* during the 1979–1980 season.

C. Long before he butted heads with the "Soup Nazi," this comic was booked on *Battlestars* as a celebrity guest.

D. In 1961 this tough-talking actor made a guest appearance on the game show *It Could Be You.*

E. Before he acted on *Saturday Night Live* or *The Simpsons,* this comedian put his voice to the test as an announcer on a 1983 game show called *The Pop 'N' Rocker Game.*

F. This Oscar-nominated actor was the host of the game show *College Mad House* from 1989–1990.

G. When this heartthrob actor was very young he appeared on a game show called *Fun House.* As part of the competition, he was asked to go fishing in a very small pool of water—the catch: he could use only his teeth to grab the fish.

Answers on page 251.

Clint Eastwood making one of his rare game show appearances back in 1961 on *It Could Be You.* At the time Clint was starring in *Rawhide.*

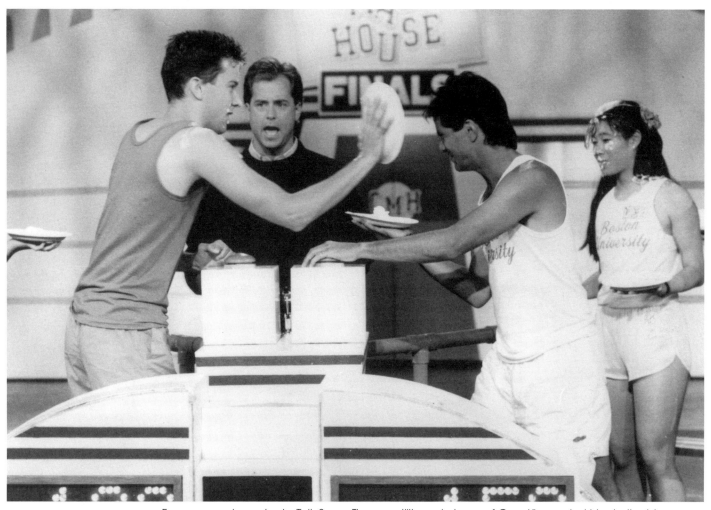

From game show pies to *Talk Soup*. The versatility and charm of Greg Kinnear led him to the big screen.

Three Funny Men
Who All
Hosted the
Same Game Show

1. **Bill Cosby**
2. **Buddy Hackett**
3. **Groucho Marx**

Can you name the show?

Answer on page 251.

Groucho never won an Academy Award for his movie antics, however, his role as the one and only Groucho on this game show won him an Emmy in 1950.

Disco Duck? Daffy Duck? No, it's Leonard the Duck from the 1980 Buddy Hackett version.

Ten Unforgettable
Game Show
Tag Lines

1. "Help control the pet population. Have your pet spayed or neutered."
   —Bob Barker, *The Price Is Right*

2. "For now, Dick Clark ... so long."—Dick Clark, *Pyramid*

3. "When you visit our sponsors, don't forget to tell'em Groucho sent ya."
   —Groucho Marx, *You Bet Your Life*

4. "Remember, it's not what you say that counts, it's what You Don't Say!"
   —Tom Kennedy, *You Don't Say!*

5. "This is Bud Collyer saying goodnight and don't you forget To Tell the Truth."—Bud Collyer, *To Tell the Truth*

6. "This is Bob Barker, hoping all your consequences are happy ones."
   —Bob Barker, *Truth or Consequences*

7. "Bye, bye. And I hope you always get the date that you really want."
   —Jim Lange, *The Dating Game*

8. "Maybe next time will be your time to Beat the Clock."
   —Bud Collyer, *Beat the Clock*

9. "The password for today is ... "
   —Allen Ludden, *Password*

10. "Love ya out there ... see ya here on the Feud."
    —Richard Dawson, *Family Feud*

Fun Fact

On the very first *Family Feud,* July 12, 1976, the Moseley family took on the Abramowitz family. The first question played was "Name a famous George." The six most popular replies of the survey of 100 people were: "George Washington" (74), "George Burns" (4), "George Gobel" (4), "George Jessel" (3), "Gorgeous George" (2), and "George Wallace" (2). It only took 200 points to win the match. The Moseley family won the feud and collected $890 in fast money.

Jim Lange and happy-luck daters say, "Bye, bye. And I hope you always get the date you really want."

Eight Guest
Wheel of Fortune
Letter Turners

1. Summer Bartholmew
2. Vicki McCarty
3. Arte Johnson
4. Tricia Gist
5. Rosie O'Donnell
6. Pat Sajak
7. Mrs. Pat Sajak
8. Betty White

Betty White not only turned letters on *Wheel of Fortune*. She also turned a few heads on *Just Men!* Betty was the first female to win an Emmy for Outstanding Game Show Host.

There's absolutely no truth to the rumor that Arte had to stand on an apple crate to turn the top row of letters on *Wheel of Fortune*.

Four *Today Show* Talents Who Kept Their Morning Duties while Hosting Game Shows

1. **Hugh Downs**
2. **Joe Garagolia**
3. **Jack Lescoulie**
4. **Al Roker**

Can you match the *Today Show* talents with the game shows they hosted?

A. *He Said, She Said*
B. *Concentration*
C. *Remember This?*
D. *Brains & Brawn*

Answers on page 251.

Fun Facts

Hugh Downs began his career as a staff announcer for NBC in Chicago in 1943 after serving in the U.S. Army. He transferred to New York in 1954 to join Arlene Francis and the *Home* show. In July 1957 he joined Jack Paar as his sidekick on *The Tonight Show*. When Paar left *The Tonight Show* in 1962, Downs moved over to host *Today* for nine years. In 1985 Downs was recognized by the *Guinness Book of World Records* for holding the record for the greatest number of hours on network commercial television.

The original set for *Sale of the Century* had to be sawed in half before it was placed on stage at NBC in New York. The original pilot for the show was taped in Los Angeles, but due to a lack of studio space, the show was moved to NBC Studio 8H at Rockefeller Center in New York. According to set designer Ed Flesh, the set was too large for the elevator that would take it to the stage where the show was to be taped.

Three Landmarks for Chuck Barris Productions

1965   Chuck Barris sells *The Dating Game,* hosted by Jim Lange, to the ABC daytime lineup. By 1966, the show goes prime time.

1966   Barris strikes gold again on ABC with the sale of *The Newlywed Game,* hosted by Bob Eubanks. Like its sister show, *The Dating Game, The Newlywed Game* had a successful eight-year run on ABC daytime and four years on ABC prime time, and it has flourished in syndication into the new millennium.

1976   *The Gong Show* comes to television and takes America by storm. Chuck Barris hosted the NBC daytime version, and both Gary Owens and Chuck Barris hosted the syndicated version.

No, that's not James Bond on the left, that's secret agent Chuck Barris. At least according to his autobiography, *Confessions of a Dangerous Mind*. With Chuck is Jim Lange.

In this nighttime version of *The Gong Show,* the lovely Siv Aberg presents a trophy and a check totaling $712.05 to the winner.

Fifteen Game Show Hosts and Their Spouses Who Appeared on *Tattletales*

1. Steve Allen and Jayne Meadows
2. Bill and Becky Anderson
3. Bob and Dorothy Jo Barker
4. Bert and Ann Convy
5. Bill and Ann Cullen
6. Monty and Marilyn Hall
7. Dennis and Micki James
8. Vicki Lawrence and Al Schultz
9. Allen Ludden and Betty White
10. Wink and Sandy Martindale
11. Jan and Toni Murray
12. Jack and Doroles Narz
13. Gene and Helen Rayburn
14. Bobby Van and Elaine Joyce
15. Chuck Woolery and Jo Ann Pflug

With every successful man is a great woman behind the man and supporting him with all her heart. That was Ann Cullen.

Wink and Sandy first met in 1972 while Wink was hosting his hit CBS game show *Gambit*. They've been together ever since.

133

52 Forty-one Game Shows from One Packager (a record achievement by Mark Goodson/Goodson-Todman)

1. *Beat the Clock*
2. *The Better Sex*
3. *Blockbusters*
4. *Body Language*
5. *By Popular Demand*
6. *Call My Bluff*
7. *Card Sharks*
8. *Child's Play*
9. *Choose up Sides*
10. *Classic Concentration*
11. *Concentration*
12. *Double Dare*
13. *Family Feud*
14. *Get the Message*
15. *He Said, She Said*
16. *It's News to Me*
17. *I've Got a Secret*
18. *Judge for Yourself*
19. *Make the Connection*
20. *The Match Game*
21. *Mindreaders*
22. *Missing Links*
23. *The Name's the Same*
24. *Now You See It*
25. *Number Please*
26. *Password*
27. *Password Plus*
28. *Play Your Hunch*
29. *The Price Is Right*
30. *Say When!*
31. *Showoffs*
32. *Snap Judgment*
33. *Split Personality*
34. *Super Password*
35. *Tattletales*
36. *To Tell the Truth*
37. *Trivia Trap*
38. *Two for the Money*
39. *What's Going On?*
40. *What's My Line?*
41. *Winner Take All*

Trivia Trap capitalized on the "Trivial Pursuit" craze of the 1980s. This was Bob Eubanks's third show for ABC.

Fun Fact

In the fall of 1969, **Beat the Clock** was received as a first-run syndicated series with the addition of a celebrity guest each week to help the contestants. The first year the show was taped in New York City, then it moved production to Montreal, Canada, for the remaining four years. **Beat the Clock** was the only Mark Goodson game show ever to be produced in Canada.

Jack Narz says, "Allen, the password is … 'laundry.' All you have to do is take off all of your clothes, put them in the laundry basket and … "

53

Nine Game Show Hosts Who Were Top-40 Radio Disc Jockeys

1. **Geoff Edwards**
2. **Bob Eubanks**
3. **Art James**
4. **Casey Kasem**
5. **Jim Lange**
6. **Wink Martindale**
7. **Gary Owens**
8. **Jim Perry**
9. **Ryan Seacrest**

Multi-talented Wink Martindale proves he's not just a game show host. In 1959 he had a top, million-seller titled "Deck of Cards." Wink is currently heard on more than 200 radio stations with his award-winning radio show, *The Music of Your Life.* Visit his Web site at www.winkmartindale.com.

Fun Fact

In 1976, in addition to hosting *The Gong Show,* Gary Owens was also hosting a nationally syndicated radio show, as well as his own top-rated daily radio show at station KMPC in California. In 1994 and 1995, Gary Owens was inducted into three national Broadcasting Halls of Fame, joining such legends as Jack Benny, Carol Burnett, George Burns, Walter Cronkite, Red Skelton, and Orson Welles. Gary Owens is one of the most successful radio legends and animation voices of all time. He is currently heard on more than 200 radio stations with *The Music of Your Life* as well as many television campaigns and national commercials for both radio and television. He's even featured on a slot machine with fellow emcee Bob Eubanks. A true icon!

54 Three Game Show Hosts Who Appeared as Celebrity Contestants on *Jeopardy!* with Art Fleming

1. Bill Cullen
2. Art James
3. Peter Marshall

Bill Cullen chuckles as Art James tries to hornswaggle Art Fleming with an incorrect answer.

Could life be any better ... Art Fleming hosted *Jeopardy!* for eleven glorious years on NBC.

Twelve Hit Songs from Game Show Personalities

1. "Just a Gigolo"
2. "The Night the Lights Went out in Georgia"
3. "If I Knew You Were Coming, I'd've Baked a Cake"
4. "Take Good Care of Her"
5. "16 Tons"
6. "I've Got a Lovely Bunch of Coconuts"
7. "Black Denim Trousers"
8. "We Love You, Call Collect"
9. "Deck of Cards"
10. "Palisade Park"
11. "Still"
12. "Naturally Stoned"

Can you match up these celebrities with their popular songs from above?

A. Bill Anderson
B. Chuck Barris (writer)
C. Eileen Barton
D. Bert Convy
E. Tennessee Ernie Ford
F. Merv Griffin
G. Vicki Lawrence
H. Art Linkletter
 I. Jaye P. Morgan
J. Adam Wade
K. Chuck Woolery (writer)
L. Wink Martindale

Answers on page 251.

Art Linkletter looks at Bert Convy and says, "Mine's bigger than yours ... hit song that is."

Win, Lose or Draw's Vicki Lawrence has had a wonderful life thanks to Carol Burnett's starting her TV career.

Ten Longest-Running
Game Shows from
Mark Goodson and
Bill Todman Productions

1. *The Price Is Right*
2. *What's My Line?*
3. *To Tell the Truth*
4. *Password*
5. *Match Game*
6. *Beat the Clock*
7. *I've Got a Secret*
8. *Family Feud*
9. *Classic Concentration*
10. *Card Sharks*

Panel shows were the forte of Goodson-Todman Productions in the early years. Mark Goodson was the master at assembling panels of class, wit, and chemistry.

The handwriting says it all, Mark Goodson was the creative genius
behind the company, and Bill Todman was the business end.

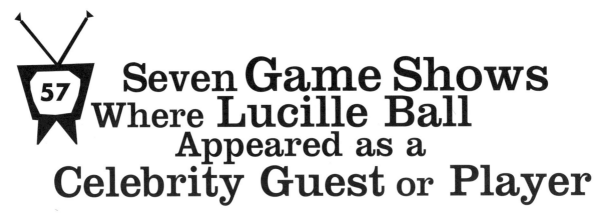

57 Seven Game Shows Where Lucille Ball Appeared as a Celebrity Guest or Player

1. *Password*
2. *Password Plus*
3. *Body Language*
4. *What's My Line?* (guest)
5. *High Rollers* (guest)
6. *I've Got a Secret* (guest)
7. *Pantomime Quiz*

Fun Fact

Lucille Ball was once quoted as saying that Alex Trebek and *High Rollers* were her favorite game show duo. She made several guest star visits to the *High Rollers* set! Lucy's personal friend Ruta Lee looks on with admiration.

That's host Tom Kennedy giving last-minute instructions to celebrity guest and comedy legend Lucille Ball. One can only imagine what thoughts were going through Lucy's mind as she prepared to put her physical comedy and pantomime genius to work. The more words a player could convey using only body language the better chance their partner had at solving the puzzle. Whenever a show needed puzzles, Steve Ryan was up to the challenge.

Three **Super** Substitute Hosts for *The $64,000 Question*

1. **Charlton Heston**
2. **Ginger Rogers**
3. **Ed Sullivan**

Ginger Rogers steps out without Fred Astaire to host *The $64,000 Question.*

Charlton Heston loved game shows and appeared on many of them. Here we see him on *Liar's Club* with Allen Ludden.

59

Four Landmarks for Merv Griffin Productions

1964   ***Jeopardy!*** with original host Art Fleming debuts on NBC.

1975   ***Wheel of Fortune*** with original host Chuck Woolery and letter turner Susan Stafford debuts on NBC.

1982   ***Wheel of Fortune*** with new host Pat Sajak and Vanna White enters into first-run syndication.

1983   ***Jeopardy!*** with new host Alex Trebek enters into first-run syndication.

Merv and one of his many Emmys from his hit shows. Donald Trump, eat your heart out.

The original team for *Wheel of Fortune,* Susan Stafford and Chuck Woolery. The chemistry was great and they led the parade for six years together.

149

Seven Contestants Who Became Game Show Hosts

1. Rudy Boesch, *Survivor* contestant
2. Mark DeCarlo, *Sale of the Century* contestant
3. Ron Maestri, *Win, Lose or Draw* contestant
4. Frank Nicotero, *Debt* contestant and *UFL: Ultimate Fan League* contestant
5. Mike Reilly, *Jeopardy!* contestant
6. Paul Reubens, *The Gong Show* contestant
7. Gene Wood, *The Generation Game* contestant

Can you match the contestants with the game shows they hosted?

A. *Monopoly*
B. *You Don't Know Jack*
C. *Street Smarts*
D. *Combat Missions*
E. *Quicksilver*
F. *Studs* and *Big Deal*
G. *Beat the Clock* and *Anything You Can Do*

Answers on page 252.

Frank Nicotero had the smarts to win big on *Debt* with Wink Martindale.

"You know Gene, my girl couldn't bake an apple pie but she could make a banana cream."

151

Twenty **Academy** Award– Winning Best Actors Who Appeared as Mystery Guests on *What's My Line?*

Actor	Film	Date of Appearance
Yul Brenner	*The King and I*	1/6/57
James Cagney	*Yankee Doodle Dandy*	5/15/60
Art Carney	*Harry and Tonto*	5/16/64
Gary Cooper	*Sergeant York, High Noon*	10/18/59
Jose Ferrer	*Cyrano de Bergerac*	6/26/55
Peter Finch	*Network*	8/13/68
Henry Fonda	*On Golden Pond*	1/15/61
Gene Hackman	*The French Connection*	10/21/71
Charlton Heston	*Ben-Hur*	10/28/56
Dustin Hoffman	*Kramer vs. Kramer*	12/10/68
William Holden	*Stalag 17*	9/23/56
Charles Laughton	*The Private Life of Henry VIII*	11/25/56
Jack Lemmon	*Save the Tiger*	11/3/57
Frederick March	*Dr. Jekyll and Mr. Hyde*	
	The Best Years of Our Lives	3/21/54
Ray Milland	*The Lost Weekend*	10/31/54
Paul Muni	*The Story of Louis Pasteur*	8/14/55
Paul Newman	*Color of Money*	1/25/59
Cliff Robertson	*Charly*	7/30/68
James Stewart	*The Philadelphia Story*	11/10/63
John Wayne	*True Grit*	11/13/60

The panel tries to decipher which Academy® Award winner is tonight's mystery guest.

JAMES STEWART   SALLY KELLERMAN   JOHN FORSYTHE

Jimmy Stewart was a big fan of game shows and frequently made the rounds as a celebrity guest. Here he is on *The Movie Game*.

The Seven Longest-Running Game Shows in Television History

1. *The Price Is Right**, CBS daytime, thirty-three years, debuted September 1972.

2. *Wheel of Fortune**, syndicated, twenty-two years, debuted September 1983.

3. *Jeopardy!**, syndicated, twenty-one years, debuted September 1984.

4. *What's My Line?*, CBS primetime, seventeen years and seven months, debuted February 1950.

5. *Wheel of Fortune*, NBC/CBS daytime, sixteen years and nine months, debuted January 1975.

6. *I've Got a Secret*, CBS primetime, fourteen years and ten months, debuted June 1952.

7. *Concentration*, NBC daytime, fourteen years and seven months, debuted August 1958.

NOTE: * Show is still on the air.

The Cadillac of game shows, *The Price Is Right* with Bob Barker.

The time was right for another hit panel game show from Mark Goodson and Bill Todman. From left to right, that's Henry Morgan, Bill Cullen, Bess Myerson, host Garry Moore, and Betsy Palmer.

63 Three Game Shows Hosted by Wink Martindale Whose Titles Asked a Question

1. *What's This Song?*
2. *How's Your Mother-in-Law?*
3. *Can You Top This?*

Tough competition—Phyllis Diller finds Michael Landon too much as an Indian wrestler but hopes to best him in guessing song titles.

Wink asks the delicate question, *How's Your Mother-in-Law?* That's Richard Dawson, Larry Storch, and George Carlin in the hot seats on the first week of shows.

Eighteen Game Shows that Couldn't Survive the Powerhouse Ratings of Bob Barker and *The Price Is Right*

Show	Date Cancelled
Jeopardy!	January 1975
High Rollers	June 1976
Celebrity Sweepstakes	October 1976
All-Star Secrets	August 1979
Hollywood Squares	June 1980
Password Plus	March 1982
Battlestars	April 1982
Hit Man	April 1983
Battlestars	July 1983
Dream House	June 1984
Trivia Trap	April 1985
Family Feud	June 1985
All-Star Blitz	December 1985
Bruce Forsyth's Hot Streak	April 1986
Double Talk	December 1986
Bargain Hunters	September 1987
Wheel of Fortune	June 1989
Scrabble	March 1990

Fun Fact
After *Hit Man,* co-author Fred Wostbrock landed on his feet working for Merrill Heatter. Merrill, Alex, and Fred are the best of friends to this day.

Man your battle stations for the star-studded *Battlestars* starring Alex Trebek. A young unknown comic named Jerry Seinfeld was booked as a guest.

That's right ... *The Price Is Right* was the hit man that knocked this show off the air.

Fun Fact
Creator Jay Wolpert gave co-author Fred Wostbrock his first job in TV game shows. Fred was a researcher on *Hit Man.* Twenty-three years later Fred and Jay are still the best of friends.

Six Fabulous Females Who Appeared on Game Shows

1. Kirstie Alley
2. Sandra Bernhard
3. Kathy Lee Gifford
4. Meg Ryan
5. Vanna White
6. Jenny Jones

Can you match up these celebrities with the game shows they appeared on?

1. This comedienne appeared as a guest on *The $1.98 Beauty Show,* a game show in which female contestants of all ages competed in mock beauty contests.

2. This famous game show assistant didn't originally start out turning letters. She first appeared on *The Price Is Right* as a contestant and never made it out of contestant row.

3. In 1980—long before her *Cheers* fame—this actress was a contestant on *Password Plus* and won $800.

4. She appeared as a contestant on the CBS hit game show *Press Your Luck* long before she was a talk show queen.

5. Before starring in her morning talk show with Regis Philbin, she was a vocalist on *Name That Tune.*

6. This actress, then featured in the daytime soap *As the World Turns,* appeared in 1983 as part of a showcase skit on *The Price Is Right.*

Answers on page 252.

Kirstie Alley's roots have always been in show business. Even as a contestant on *Password Plus* she introduced herself as an aspiring actress.

Here's the story of a lovely lady ... she appears as a contestant on *The Price Is Right* and loses, and then she lands the best female role in game show history. Get serious, it couldn't happen in a million years ... but it did for Vanna.

Six Game Show Titles that Were Recycled for Thirteen Completely Different Shows

1. *Break the Bank*—1948, 1976, 1985
2. *Chance of a Lifetime*—1950, 1952
3. *Double Dare*—1976, 1986
4. *Strike It Rich*—1951, 1986
5. *The Perfect Match*—1967, 1994
6. *Wheel of Fortune*—1952, 1975

Check out the *Encyclopedia of TV Game Shows* for a complete description of each show.

Fun Fact
Tom Kennedy hosted the ABC version and Jack Barry hosted 1976's syndicated version of *Break the Bank.*

With Bert Parks's head of hair, Vitalis and Brill Creme (the giant tube seen over Bert's shoulder) were the perfect sponsors for *Break the Bank*. Without a doubt Bert Parks used more than just a little dab.

Two Game Shows
that Have Aired in Six Different Decades

1. *The Price Is Right*
2. *To Tell the Truth*

Both shows debuted in 1956.
Both shows were created by Bob Stewart for Mark Goodson and Bill Todman.

Bob Stewart created this original version of *The Price Is Right* for Mark Goodson and Bill Todman. This marked the first time that Bill Cullen and Bob Stewart would work together. Over the years, Bob hired Bill to host eight of his show creations.

Fun Fact
Merv Griffin, Jack Narz, and Arlene Francis were all guest hosts while Bill Cullen was on vacation.

Let the good times roll. Bob Barker and Rod Roddy *celebrate nineteen years of* The Price Is Right *on CBS daytime back in 1991. Not even the producers could have foreseen the show's juggernaut success that continues into the 21st century.*

Thirteen Celebrities Who Were Once Unknown Contestants on Game Shows

1. Tom Brokaw, *Two for the Money*
2. Dr. Joyce Brothers, *The $64,000 Question*
3. Leonardo DiCaprio, *Fun House*
4. Phyllis Diller, *You Bet Your Life*
5. Mel Harris, *The $20,000 Pyramid*
6. Jenny Jones, *Match Game* and *Press Your Luck*
7. Naomi Judd, *Hollywood Squares* and *Password*
8. Kathy Najimy, *Family Feud* and *Wheel of Fortune*
9. Robert Redford, *Play Your Hunch*
10. John Ritter, *The Dating Game*
11. Tom Selleck, *The Dating Game*
12. O.J. Simpson, *Hollywood Squares*
13. Vanna White, *The Price Is Right*

The winning moment! Host Hal March looks on as contestant Dr. Joyce Brothers wins $64,000. Strangely her expertise in boxing won her the top prize.

Here she is ... the First Lady of Stand-Up ... Phyllis Diller. It was her appearance on *You Bet Your Life* that jump-started her comedy career.

Four Landmarks for Jack Barry and Dan Enright Productions

1940s   Radio emcee Jack Barry teams up with producer Dan Enright. They create *Juvenile Jury* and *Life Begins at 80,* among other shows.

1950s   The team enters the television game show arena with such creations as *High Low, Twenty-One,* and *Tic Tac Dough.*

1956   Jack Barry hosts *Twenty-One,* a show that he and partner Dan Enright create for NBC. This show would later be implicated in the quiz show scandals.

1957   Charles Van Doren makes his contestant debut on *Twenty-One* winning a grand total of $129,000. In August of this year, *Look* magazine breaks the first story about the scandals. By October of the following year *Twenty-One* is canceled and the team of Barry and Enright breaks up ... until the mid '70s when they make a comeback with *The Joker's Wild* and *Tic Tac Dough.*

The creative team of Jack Barry and Dan Enright was blackballed because of the quiz show scandals of the 1950s. They would resurface some twenty years later with two mega-hits, *The Joker's Wild* and *Tic Tac Dough*.

Fun Fact
While hosting *Tic Tac Dough*, Jack Barry hosted *Twenty-One* and *High Low* in the same year and all for NBC.

Seven *Playboy* Centerfolds Who Became Game Show Models, Assistants, and Co-Hosts

1. Julie Ciani
2. Heather Kozar
3. Jenny McCarthy
4. Gena Lee Nolin
5. Ann Pennington
6. Janice Pennington
7. Nikki Ziering

Can you name the game shows on which they appeared and who was the first to break the nudity barrier?

Answers on page 252.

175

I'm sure you'd like to see them all naked in *Playboy*, excluding Rod and Bob, of course. From left to right we see Kathleen Bradley, Janice Pennington, Holly Halstrom, and Gena Lee Nolin. Only Janice and Gena took it all off.

You've heard of Barker's Beauties ... meet Perry's Pinups. That's Ann Pennington on the left and Janice Baker on the right. It was Ann who bared all in *Playboy*.

Nine Game Show Hosts Who Were Guest Stars on *Batman*

1. Jack Bailey
2. Jack Barry
3. Dick Clark
4. Steve Dunne
5. Dennis James
6. Jack Kelly
7. Art Linkletter
8. Allen Ludden
9. Gary Owens

"Hi Adam, my name is Dennis James. I'm a very famous game show host. I'd like to audition for the role of Quizzler."

The password is ... "cameo." And that's just what Allen Ludden did on the classic *Batman* series back in 1966.

Thirteen Game Shows on Which Adam West Appeared as a Celebrity Guest

1. *The Dating Game*, 1966
2. *Your All-American College Show*, 1967
3. *Hollywood Squares*, 1969
4. *Password*, 1971
5. *Family Feud*, 1977
6. *Scattergories*, 1993
7. *Pictionary*, 1997
8. *Happy Hour*, 1999
9. *TV Land Ultimate Fan Search*, 2000
10. *Singled Out*, 2000
11. *I've Got a Secret*, 2001
12. *Who Wants to Be a Millionaire*, 2001
13. *Hollywood Squares*, 2002

Fun Fact

As a kid growing up in New Jersey, co-author Fred Wostbrock would watch reruns of *Batman,* on WPIX-TV every day. Some twenty years later his childhood dream came true: Fred became Adam West's agent!

Excellent clue, Adam. But our word authority, Dr. Reason A. Goodwin, has determined that "Gotham" is a proper noun.

Fun Fact

The dynamic duo of Allen Ludden and Betty White were good friends of Adam West's. Adam asked Betty to appear in his 2003 CBS movie of the week, *Return to the Batcave.*

Fun Fact

Adam West served as co-host for an entire episode of *Singled Out* that was themed around his classic series *Batman.* In a fun skit, Adam had to save both emcee Chris Hardwick (pictured) and co-host Carmen Electra. Randall Malone (pictured) also appeared in the skit.

73

Three Game Show Personalities Who Posed Nude for *Cosmopolitan* Magazine

1. **John Davidson, host**
2. **Burt Reynolds, creator, producer**
3. **Lyle Waggoner, host**

John Davidson says, "Eat your heart out Burt. Mine's bigger than yours is ... smile that is!"

Burt Reynolds was certainly no "square." He was the first man to pose nude for *Cosmopolitan* magazine.

Nine **Box Games** that Became **TV Game Shows**

1. *Boggle*, hosted by Wink Martindale
2. *Jumble,* hosted by Wink Martindale
3. *Madlibs,* hosted by David Sidoni
4. *Monopoly,* hosted by Michael Reilly
5. *Pictionary,* first version hosted by Brian Robbins, second version hosted by Alan Thicke
6. *Scattergories,* hosted by Dick Clark
7. *Scrabble,* hosted by Chuck Woolery
8. *Taboo,* hosted by Chris Wylde
9. *Trivial Pursuit,* hosted by Wink Martindale

Two fun-filled game shows that required some brains to play. Who better than Chuck and Dick to host the festivities?

In 1994 Wink Martindale managed to license, executive produce, and host the hottest box game since *Monopoly*.

Two Game Shows Where We Never Saw the Host's Face

1. *100%*—Casey Kasem was never seen at all.
2. *Inquizition*—The Inquizitor was only seen from the backside.

Fun Fact
It was part of the Inquizitor's contract that his true identity would never be known.

Is it Santa Claus, Kenny Rogers, Father Time, or none of the above? None of the above is correct. He's the Inquizitor.

Legendary broadcaster Casey Kasem with his top agent, Don Pitts, at a recording session for *100%*.

Fun Fact

Hollywood agent Don Pitts handled the voice-over careers of these superstars: Casey Kasem, Tom Kennedy, Peter Marshall, Wink Martindale, Gary Owens, and Adam West, among others.

Twenty-one Game Shows
that Went to Pilot with One Host and Went to Series with Another Host

Show	Pilot Host	Series Host
3rd Degree	Peter Marshall	Bert Convy
3's a Crowd	Wink Martindale	Jim Peck
50 Grand Slam	Peter Haskell	Tom Kennedy
Blackout	Robb Weller	Bob Goen
Catch Phrase	Rick Barry	Art James
Hollywood Game	Peter Allen	Bob Goen
Holllywood's Talking	Al Lohman	Geoff Edwards
Make Me Laugh	Geoff Edwards	Bobby Van
Match Game (1990)	Bert Convy	Ross Shafer
Movie Game	Jack Narz	Sonny Fox
Show-Offs	Larry Blyden	Bobby Van
The Joker's Wild	Allen Ludden	Jack Barry
To Tell the Truth	Mike Wallace	Bud Collyer
To Tell the Truth (1990)	Richard Kline	Gordon Elliott
Two for the Money	Fred Allen	Herb Shriner
Wheel of Fortune	Edd Byrnes	Chuck Woolery
Who, What or Where Game	Jack Narz	Art James
Winning Streak	Art James	Bill Cullen
Wordplay	Peter Tomarken	Tom Kennedy
Your Number's Up	Geoff Edwards	Nipsey Russell

The witty and loveable Larry Blyden died an untimely death in Morocco shortly after this pilot was taped.

Bobby Van got the nod to replace Larry Blyden, when the show suffered Blyden's untimely death after only twenty-six weeks.

Seven Network Pages Who Became Game Show Hosts

1. Chuck Barris, NBC
2. Bill Leyden, NBC
3. Peter Marshall, NBC
4. Regis Philbin, NBC
5. Gene Rayburn, NBC
6. Marc Summers, CBS
7. Gene Wood, NBC

Young ...

... And younger. Both of these whipper snappers went on to achieve game show stardom.

78

Six Game Show Hosts
Who Were Panelist on
Liar's Club

1. **Bill Cullen**
2. **Bob Eubanks**
3. **Tom Kennedy**
4. **Peter Marshall**
5. **Jim McKrell**
6. **Betty White**

Bob Eubanks catches the celebrity panel totally off guard when he comments on the mystery object.

Fun Fact
Liar's Club made its debut in 1969 with **Twilight Zone** host Rod Serling as emcee.

You may remember Larry Hovis as Carter from *Hogan's Heros*. Also seen here are Alan Sues from Broadway and *Laugh-in* fame, Dody Goodman from *Mary Hartman, Mary Hartman,* and the ever-popular Bill Cullen.

Four Landmarks for Ralph Edwards Productions

1940   *Truth or Consequences* begins on radio with creator Ralph Edwards as host.

1950   *Truth or Consequences* begins its first of many television runs throughout the '50s, '60s, '70s, and '80s.

1956   Ralph Edwards replaces himself with Bob Barker as the new host of *Truth or Consequences*. This would mark Barker's game show hosting debut.

1974   *Name That Tune* takes America by storm in both daytime and prime time.

Ralph Edwards, the show's creator serves as grand marshall of the *Truth or Consequences* New Mexico parade and festival.

I can name that legendary host in two notes ... Tom Kennedy.

80

Eight Classic Game Show Hosts Who Have Played for Charity on *Card Sharks*

1. Jack Clark
2. Bill Cullen
3. Tom Kennedy
4. Jim Lange
5. Allen Ludden
6. Wink Martindale
7. Gene Rayburn
8. Alex Trebek

Jim Perry presents the Four Aces. No, not the singers ... four of the best game show hosts in the business.

In a second week of charity games, Jim Perry introduces four more greats of the game show world.

Five Game Shows on Which David Letterman Has Appeared as a Guest Star

1. *The Gong Show*
2. *Liar's Club*
3. *The Love Experts*
4. *Password Plus*
5. *The $20,000 Pyramid*

Fun Fact

Before becoming a phenomenon as a late-night talk show host, David Letterman tried his hand at hosting his own game shows. In 1977, he emceed a Bob Stewart creation called *The Riddlers.* The show never became a series. Lucky for David, because a few years later he found his true calling.

Allen Ludden is proud to present the son he always wanted … David Letterman.

Chuck Barris always put a little dab of Alpo on his crotch prior to doing a dog act on *The Gong Show*.

82

Two Times when Mark Goodson Hosted His Own Game Show Creations

1. *To Tell the Truth* in 1967 when he filled in for Bud Collyer.
2. Twenty-four years later, once again on *To Tell the Truth* on February 19, 1991 when he filled in for Alex Trebek, who was rushed to the hospital when his wife gave birth to their first child.

Mark Goodson was no stranger to the microphone. He began his show business career as a disc jockey at a San Francisco radio station.

Tom Poston asks the great Mark Goodson, "Are you sure the show must go on ... Peggy Cass hasn't arrived yet!"

Eight Emcees Who Created Game Shows They Hosted

1. Chuck Barris (with Chris Beard), *The Gong Show*
2. Jack Barry (with Dan Enright), *Twenty-One, Tic Tac Dough, Concentration, High Low, The Joker's Wild, Joker! Joker! Joker!,* and *Break the Bank* (1976)
3. Bob Eubanks (with Michael Hill), *All-Star Secrets*
4. Merv Griffin, *Word for Word*
5. Monty Hall (with Stefan Hatos), *Let's Make a Deal, It's Anybody's Guess,* and *Split Second*
6. Wink Martindale (with Bill Hillier excluding *Headline Chasers*), *Headline Chasers, Trivial Pursuit, Boggle, Jumble,* and *Shuffle*
7. Jan Murray, *Treasure Hunt* and *Charge Account*
8. Mike Stokey, *Pantomime Quiz* and *Stump the Stars*

Fun Fact
Arnold Schwarzenegger was a guest on *All-Star Secrets* in 1979.

Fun Fact
The original pilot for *The Joker's Wild* was taped in 1969 with Allen Ludden as emcee.

84

Three Questions Groucho Marks Asked to Losing Contestants on *You Bet Your Life*

1. Who was buried in Grant's tomb?
2. How much does a five-cent cigar cost?
3. What was the color of Napoleon's white horse?

Here we see Groucho Marx and announcer/sidekick George Fenneman holding the show's quiz questions, which progressed in difficulty as the dollar amounts increased. Groucho hated to see contestants go home empty handed. He used quirky questions to assure that losers went home with some money.

206

"If you say Napoleon's white horse was black you'll get no argument from me."

Seven Game Shows that Mike Wallace Hosted before He Joined *60 Minutes* in 1968

1. *The Big Surprise*
2. *Guess Again*
3. *I'll Buy That*
4. *Majority Rules*
5. *There's One in Every Family*
6. *Who Pays?*
7. *Who's the Boss?*

Bonus Fact
Mike Wallace hasn't hosted a game show since he joined *60 Minutes.*

Fun Fact
Before Betsy Palmer (not seen in photo) was a panelist on *I've Got a Secret,* she was the featured model on *I'll Buy That* with Mike Wallace in 1953.

By the look on housekeeper Pat Schofield's face, one might wonder if Mike Wallace is playing footsie instead of *Who Pays?*

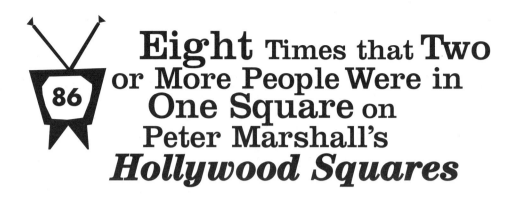

Eight Times that Two or More People Were in One Square on Peter Marshall's *Hollywood Squares*

1. **Donny and Marie**
2. **The Monkees (minus Peter Tork)**
3. **The Hudson Brothers**
4. **Paul Winchell and Jerry Mahoney**
5. **Chad and Jeremy**
6. **Dino, Desi, and Billy**
7. **Peaches and Herb**
8. **Seals and Croft**

Mickey Dolenz, Davey Jones, and Mike Nesmith join Peter Marshall on the set of *Hollywood Squares* with *Laugh-In* cast members Jo Anne Worley, Judy Carne, and Henry Gibson.

DONNY & MARIE OSMOND

The only brother and sister team to appear in the same square on *Hollywood Squares!*

Two **Emcees** with
Superstar Connections

1. Bob Eubanks—The Beatles
2. Wink Martindale—Elvis Presley

Bonus Facts

Bob Eubanks was one of LA's top radio personalities on KRLA. In 1964 Bob mortgaged his home for $20,000 to bring the Beatles to America to play at the famed Hollywood Bowl.

Wink was the top radio/TV personality on WHBQ in Memphis, Tennessee, during the 1950s. Wink was in the studio at WHBQ radio the night the very first Elvis Presley record ("That's All Right Mama") was ever played. Wink and Elvis were friends until Elvis's untimely death in 1977.

Bob Eubanks presents the Beatles at a press conference at his Studio City nightclub, the Cinnamon Cinder, in 1964 to promote their first concert on the West Coast at the Hollywood Bowl.

Local boys make good. Elvis Presley appears on Wink Martindale's *Dance Party* at TV station WHBQ in Memphis, Tennessee. Neither Elvis nor Wink had yet achieved national fame.

88 Seven Singers
Who Were Asked to "Enter and Sign in Please" on *What's My Line?*

1. **Bobby Darin**
2. **Judy Garland**
3. **Dean Martin**
4. **Frank Sinatra**
5. **Barbra Streisand**
6. **Diana Ross and The Supremes**
7. **Frank Zappa**

Mystery guests Diana Ross and The Supremes meet panel members after a playful round of *What's My Line?* in 1966.

That's one down and nine to go as Frank Sinatra is all smiles with the first round of questions.

Thirteen Unlikely
Game Show Hosts

1. Don Adams, ***Don Adams Screen Test***
2. Milton Berle, ***Jackpot Bowling***
3. Drew Carey, ***Whose Line Is It Anyway?***
4. Bill Cosby, ***You Bet Your Life***
5. Walter Cronkite, ***It's News to Me***
6. Jackie Gleason, ***You're in the Picture***
7. Donny Osmond, ***Pyramid***
8. Maury Povich, ***Twenty-One***
9. Vincent Price, ***E.S.P.***
10. Rice Brothers, ***That Quiz Show***
11. Hal Sparks, ***Treasure Mall***
12. Ryan Seacrest, ***Wild Animal Games, Click!,*** and ***Gladiators 2000***
13. Dick Van Dyke, ***Laugh Line*** and ***Mother's Day***

Fun Fact

Laugh Line, would be the last game show that Dick Van Dyke would host. Soon after *Laugh Line,* he reached superstar status with *The Dick Van Dyke Show* and *Mary Poppins.*

Long before *American Idol,* Ryan Seacrest hosted three game shows. Here he is on *Wild Animal Games.*

90 Six Celebrities Who Masqueraded as Their Famous TV Characters on *Storybook Squares*

1. Don Adams as Maxwell Smart from *Get Smart*
2. Barbara Eden as Jeannie from *I Dream of Jeannie*
3. Arte Johnson as German Soldier from *Laugh-In*
4. Carolyn Jones as Mortisha Addams from *The Addams Family*
5. Michael Landon as Little Joe from *Bonanza*
6. William Shatner as Captain Kirk from *Star Trek*

That's Joan Rivers, Charo, Roddy McDowell, and William Shatner as Captain Kirk.

219

Five time Emmy award–winner Peter Marshall introduces Michael Landon as Little Joe Cartwright from *Bonanza*.

91 Four U.S. Presidents Who Were on Game Shows before Entering and Signing in at the White House

1. Jimmy Carter, *What's My Line?*
2. Gerald Ford, *What's My Line?*
3. Richard Nixon, *Your First Impression*
4. Ronald Reagan, *Celebrity Game, I've Got a Secret,* and *What's My Line?*

Fun Fact
Richard Nixon, then running for governor of California, made an appearance in 1962 on *Your First Impression.* (Here we see an episode from 1964.)

221

Garry Moore senses greatness. Backstage at *I've Got a Secret,* Ronald Reagan whispers in his ear, "Someday I'll be president."

92 Two Game Show Hosts
Who Died while Their Popular Series Were Still on the Air

1. Allen Ludden, *Password Plus*
2. Jack Barry, *The Joker's Wild*

Once again, the show must go on. This time Jim Peck and Bill Cullen carried on the hosting duties of *The Joker's Wild*.

The show must go on. They were big shoes to fill but Bill Cullen and Tom Kennedy did a splendid job hosting *Password Plus*.

93 Eight *To Tell the Truth* Imposters Who Later Became Famous

1. **Sissy Biggers, game show host**
2. **Suzy Chafee, Olympic skier**
3. **Lauren Hutton, model/actress**
4. **Tom Landry, football coach**
5. **George Lindsay, actor**
6. **Rod McKuen, poet**
7. **Cicely Tyson, actress**
8. **Randy West, announcer**

David Ruprecht finds his buns in the shopping cart of announcer Randy West on the set of *Supermarket Sweep.*

Sissy Biggers was really hot stuff as the host of *Ready Set Cook.*

94 Sixteen Lottery Game Shows from Jonathan Goodson Productions

1. *The Big Spin* for California Lottery
2. *Bingo-Lotto* for Lithuania Lottery
3. *Bonus Bonanza* for Massachusetts Lottery
4. *A Chance de Ouro* for Brazil Lottery
5. *Flamingo Fortune* for Florida Lottery
6. *Illinois Luckiest* for Illinois Lottery
7. *Instant Riches* for Illinois Lottery
8. *New York Wired* for New York Lottery
9. *PowerBall: The Game Show* for Multi-State Lottery
10. *Second Chance Sweepstakes* for Ohio Lottery
11. *Super Cash Sweepstakes* for Iowa Lottery
12. *Telelotto* for Estonia Lottery
13. *Telemazli* for Hungary Lottery
14. *Win'n Spin* for South Africa Lottery
15. *Zama Zama* for South Africa Lottery
16. *25th Anniversary Game Show* for Pennsylvania Lottery

Fun Facts

Did you know ... co-author of this book Steve Ryan is senior games executive at Goodson's lottery division. Some of his many creations for these lottery shows include "Beach Ball," "Camelot's Riches," "Capsize," "Coney Island Coast," "Force Field," "Gold Rush," "High Roller," "Knockout," "Niagara," "PowerBall Express," "Skyscraper," "Splashdown," "Steeple Chase," "Thunderball," "Treasure Quest," "Vortex," "Wrecking Ball," and "Zero Gravity."

Jonathan Goodson has the distinction of being the most successful creator and producer of lottery game shows in television history.

Steve Ryan on the set of *Illinois Instant Riches* with "Knockout." The mysterious cube is first energized and then released into the arena for thirty seconds. It shakes, rattles, and rolls in a surprising and unpredictable manner. Should a contestant's colored cylinder survive the wacky attack, he or she could go home with instant riches of up to $100,000.

Popeye flexes his muscles for Steve on the set of *Flamingo Fortune* taped at Universal Studios in Orlando. In "Beach Ball," Popeye's muscle is needed to retrieve and reset a forty-pound beach ball that swings back and forth through a revolving turntable of giant sand castles. The more castles a player leaves standing, the greater the winnings.

Five Game Show
Announcers Who Were
Praised as the Best by *TV Guide*

1. Johnny Olson
2. Don Pardo
3. Johnny Gilbert
4. Gene Wood
5. Jay Stewart

... And Seven More that the Authors
Praise as the Best TV Has to Offer

1. John Harlan
2. Bob Hilton
3. Johnny Jacobs
4. Charlie O'Donnell
5. Rod Roddy
6. Bill Wendell
7. Kenny Williams

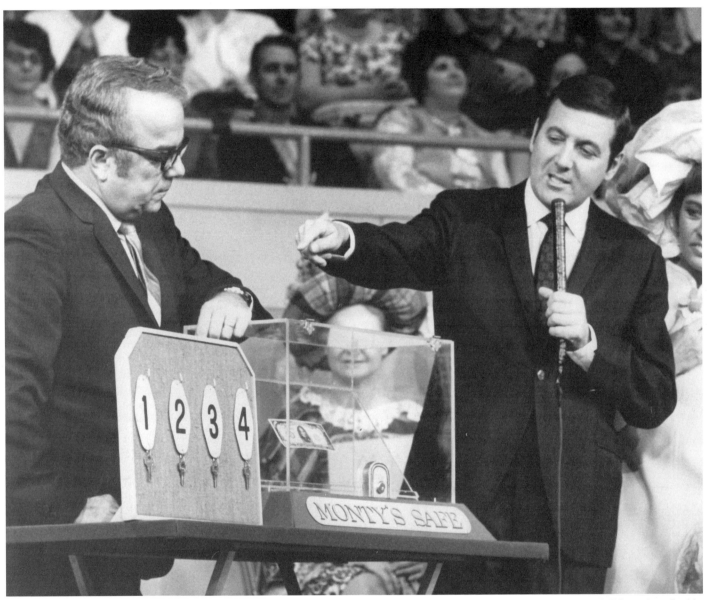

The loveable Jay Stewart, best known as Monty Hall's sidekick on *Let's Make a Deal,* was also a game show agent. When Jay died in 1989, Fred Wostbrock was recruited to carry on for Jay.

Charlie O'Donnell is recognized as one of the finest announcers in the business. Bill Cullen praises him with his gesture of admiration on the set of *The Joker's Wild*.

96 Three Game Show Hosts Who Have Hosted the Tournament of Roses Parade

1. Bill Cullen
2. Bob Eubanks
3. Betty White

Long before Betty White ever hosted a game show of her own, she co-hosted the Tournament of Roses Parade with veteran game show host Bill Cullen.

For more than two decades, Bob Eubanks has been a familiar face and voice broadcasting the Tournament of Roses Parade. Seen with Bob is co-host Stephanie Edwards.

97 Four Game Shows Wink Martindale Hosted in the Same Year
(No other host has ever hosted this many game shows in a single year.)

1. *Shuffle,* March 7, 1994
2. *Boggle,* March 7, 1994
3. *Jumble,* June 13, 1994
4. *Trivial Pursuit,* September 6, 1994

Wink Martindale is all set to host television's first hour-long interactive game show, *Trivial Pursuit,* in 1994.

Wink tells home viewers to join in on the interactive fun of *Boggle*.

98 One Game Show Host
Who Graced the Cover of *TV Guide*
Twice within a Four-Week Period

Bill Cullen

He first appeared on the cover of *TV Guide*'s Issue #487 on July 28, 1962, and then on the cover of Issue #490 on August 18, 1962.

It may look like Bill Cullen is doing his impression of Rodney Dangerfield but let me tell 'ya, Bill Cullen got plenty of respect from fellow hosts, producers, fans.

Bill ponders the thought, "Could I become one of America's favorite game show hosts?" Little did he know he'd become America's most beloved game show host.

99 Nineteen First-Run Original Half-Hour Game Shows from the Game Show Network (GSN)

1. *All New 3's a Crowd*
2. *Bert Ludden's Love Buffet*
3. *Cram*
4. *D.J. Games*
5. *Extreme Gong*
6. *Friend or Foe?*
7. *Hollywood Showdown*
8. *Inquizition*
9. *Jep!*
10. *Lingo*
11. *Mall Masters*
12. *National Lampoon's Funny Money*
13. *Russian Roulette*
14. *Super Decades*
15. *Throat & Neck*
16. *Trivia Track*
17. *Whammy*
18. *When Did That Happen?*
19. *Wintution*

MTV VJ Kennedy comes to game show network to host *Friend or Foe?*

It's *Whammy.* A new generation of *Press Your Luck* starring Todd Newton.

Twenty-one All-Time Favorite Game Shows of Steve Ryan
(in alphabetical order)

1. *Beat the Clock*
2. *Blockbusters*
3. *Camouflage*
4. *Concentration*
5. *Hollywood Squares*
6. *Jeopardy!*
7. *Let's Make a Deal*
8. *Liar's Club*
9. *Match Game*
10. *Name That Tune*
11. *The Newlywed Game*
12. *Password*
13. *PDQ*
14. *The Price Is Right*
15. *Seven Keys*
16. *Truth or Consequences*
17. *Video Village*
18. *What's My Line?*
19. *Wheel of Fortune*
20. *Who Wants to Be a Millionaire*
21. *You Bet Your Life*

Concentration was Steve Ryan's favorite game show growing up. Little did Steve know that someday he'd be the mastermind behind the *Classic Concentration* rebuses.

That's game show legend Bill Cullen at his best, hosting *Blockbusters*. Steve Ryan co-created this popular NBC game show for Mark Goodson early in his career. To this date, *Blockbusters* remains the most successful Goodson-produced Q & A game show. *Blockbusters* also earned Bill Cullen his second Emmy nomination for Best Game Show Host.

Sixty All-Time Favorite Game Shows of Fred Wostbrock

1. *All Star Secrets*
2. *Baffle*
3. *Beat the Clock*
4. *Big Showdown*
5. *Blankety Blanks*
6. *Break the Bank* (1976)
7. *Celebrity Sweepstakes*
8. *Chain Reaction* (1980)
9. *Cross-Wits* (1975)
10. *The Dating Game* (Jim Lange version)
11. *Debt*
12. *Diamond Head Game*
13. *Double Dare* (1976)
14. *Gambit*
15. *The Gong Show* (1976–1980)
16. *High Rollers* (1974–1976)
17. *Hitman*
18. *Hollywood Connection*
19. *Hollywood Squares* (1966–1981, 2002–2004)
20. *Hot Seat*
21. *It's Anybody's Guess*
22. *I've Got a Secret* (all versions)
23. *Jackpot* (1974–1975)
24. *Jeopardy!* (all versions)
25. *The Joker's Wild* (1972–1975)
26. *Let's Make a Deal* (Monty Hall versions)
27. *Liar's Club* (1976–1979)
28. *Love Experts*
29. *The Magnificent Marble Machine*
30. *Match Game* (Gene Rayburn versions)
31. *The Moneymaze*
32. *Name That Tune* (Tom Kennedy versions)
33. *The Neighbors*
34. *The Newlywed Game* (Bob Eubanks versions)
35. *Now You See It* (1974–1975)
36. *Pass the Buck*
37. *Password* (1971–1975)
38. *Press Your Luck*
39. *Price Is Right* (1972–current)
40. *Rhyme and Reason*
41. *Second Chance*
42. *Shoot for the Stars*
43. *Split Second* (1972–1975)
44. *Stumpers*
45. *Supermarket Sweep* (1990–current)
46. *Tattletales* (1974–1978)
47. *The $10,000 Pyramid* and *The $25,000 Pyramid*
48. *Three on a Match*
49. *Tic Tac Dough* (1978–1985)
50. *To Tell the Truth* (1969–1978)
51. *Treasure Hunt* (1973–1977)
52. *Trivial Pursuit*
53. *Truth or Consequences* (1966–1975)
54. *What's My Line?* (all versions)
55. *Wheel of Fortune* (1975–current)
56. *Whew!*
57. *Who Wants to Be a Millionaire*
58. *The Who, What or Where Game*
59. *Winning Streak*
60. *You Don't Say!* (1963–1975)

What are your all-time favorite game shows?

When Fred Wostbrock was a kid growing up in New Jersey, he would always watch the ABC daytime line up of shows. He grew up with these five classic hosts: Allen from *Password*, Tom from *Split Second*, Monty from *Let's Make a Deal*, Bob from *The Newlywed Game*, and Jim from *The Dating Game*.

That's Art, Dennis, Jack, Gene, Monty, Alex, and Peter. When you're in the presence of game show royalty it's not necessary to use last names.

What a thrill it was for Fred to appear on the *Geraldo* show with his clients and friends, Wink, Monty, and Gene.

Answers to Trivia Questions

Answers to page 12, "Unlikely Career Moves to Become Game Show Host"
1. Melvin Belli
2. Edgar Bergen
3. Al Capp
4. Leo Durocher
5. Ron Ely
6. Bruce Jenner
7. Jack Kelly
8. Gypsy Rose Lee
9. Basil Rathbone
10. Norman Lear

Answers to page 14, "The Ten Toughest Questions Posed to Charles Van Doren on *Twenty-One*"
The producers of *Twenty-One* gave these answers to Charles Van Doren preceding the shows.
1. General H.W. Halleck
2. Robert McCormick, Joseph Patterson
3. Second, Anne Boleyn, beheaded; third, Jane Seymour, died in childbirth; fourth, Anne of Cleves, divorced; fifth, Catherine Howard, beheaded
4. Eugene V. Debs
5. Susan B. Anthony, Elizabeth Cady Stanton, Lucretia Mott, Lucy Stone
6. Infant, schoolboy, lover, soldier, justice (or respectable professional man), "lean and slipper'd pantaloon" (or head of household), second childishness (or mere oblivion)
7. 1. Anton Chekhov, 2. *The Wisteria Tree,* 3. Joshua Logan, 4. Joshua Logan
8. Vice presidents: Andrew Johnson and Hannibal Hamlin; and secretaries of war: Simon Cameron and Edwin Staton
9. 1. Iran, 2. Andrei Vishinsky, 3. Edward Stettinius
10. Majorca, Minorca, Iviza, and Formentera

Answers to page 25, "Match the Classic Game Show with Its Original Title That Never Made It to the Airwaves"
1. *Nothing but the Truth* became *To Tell the Truth*
2. *Auctionaire* became *The Price Is Right*
3. *Shopper's Bazaar* became *Wheel of Fortune*
4. *What's the Question?* became *Jeopardy!*
5. *On a Roll* became *Family Feud*

Answers to page 38, "Match the Game Show with Its Popular Theme Song"
1. "A Pretty Girl Is Like a Melody," *The Big Payoff*
2. "Spanish Flea," *The Dating Game*
3. "We're in the Money," *Doctor I.Q.*
4. "Ain't She Sweet," *The $1.98 Beauty Show*
5. "A Swingin' Safari," *The Match Game*
6. "Book of Love," *The Newlywed Game* (1988)
7. "Everything's Coming up Roses," *Seven Keys*
8. "Three Blind Mice," *Your First Impression*

Answer to page 51, "Which Host Made the Pilot for *To Tell the Truth?*"
Mike Wallace

Answers to page 63, "Match the Comedians with the Game Shows They Hosted"
1. Steve Allen, *I've Got a Secret*
2. Milton Berle, *Jackpot Bowling*
3. Johnny Carson, *Earn Your Vacation*
4. Bill Cosby, *You Bet Your Life*
5. Jackie Gleason, *You're in the Picture*
6. Ernie Kovacs, *Gamble on Love*
7. Groucho Marx, *You Bet Your Life*
8. Gary Owens, *The Gong Show*
9. Carl Reiner, *Celebrity Game*
10. Rip Taylor, *The $1.98 Beauty Show*
11. Dick Van Dyke, *Laugh Line*

Answers to page 76, "Six Trivia Quiz Answers that All Begin with the Letter 'W'"
1. Woolery
2. *What's My Line?*
3. *Who Do You Trust?*
4. *What's My Line?*
5. *Wallace*
6. *Winner Take All*

Answers to page 90, "Name the Game Shows Associated with the Popular Icons"
1. Barker's Beauties—*The Price Is Right*
2. Dr. Reason A. Goodwin—*Password*
3. Whammy—*Press Your Luck*
4. The Town Crier—*Video Village*
5. Kenny the Cop—*Shenangians*
6. Beulah the Buzzer—*Truth or Consequences*
7. Edgar the Talking Jukebox—*Fandango*

Answers to page 102, "Match the Female Substitute Game Show Host with the Game Show She Hosted"
  1. Arlene Francis, *The Price Is Right*
  2. Celeste Holm, *The $64,000 Question*
  3. Ginger Rogers, *The $64,000 Question*
  4. Sally Struthers, *Win, Lose or Draw*
  5. Betty White, *Password*

Answers to page 115, "Match the Celebrities with the Game Shows They Appeared On"
  A. Johnny Carson, *Earn Your Vacation*
  B. Cuba Gooding, Jr., *The Dating Game*
  C. Jerry Seinfeld, *Battlestars*
  D. Clint Eastwood, *It Could Be You*
  E. Phil Hartman, *The Pop 'N' Rocker Game*
  F. Greg Kinnear, *College Mad House*
  G. Leonardo DiCaprio, *Fun House*

Answer to page 118, "Which Game Show Was Hosted by Bill Cosby, Buddy Hackett, and Groucho Marx?"
You Bet Your Life

Answers to page 126, "Match the *Today Show* Talents with the Game Shows They Hosted"
  1. Hugh Downs, *Concentration*
  2. Joe Garagolia, *He Said, She Said*
  3. Jack Lescoulie, *Brains & Brawn*
  4. Al Roker, *Remember This?*

Answers to page 140, "Match the Game Show Personality with Their Pop Song"
  1. "Just a Gigolo," Jaye P. Morgan (among others)
  2. "The Night the Lights Went out in Georgia," Vicki Lawrence
  3. "If I Knew You Were Coming, I'd've Baked a Cake," Eileen Barton
  4. "Take Good Care of Her," Adam Wade (among others)
  5. "16 Tons," Tennessee Ernie Ford (among others)
  6. "I've Got a Lovely Bunch of Coconuts," Merv Griffin
  7. "Black Denim Trousers," Bert Convy
  8. "We Love You, Call Collect," Art Linkletter
  9. "Deck of Cards," Wink Martindale
10. "Palisade Park," Chuck Barris
11. "Still," Bill Anderson (among others)
12. "Naturally Stoned," Chuck Woolery

Answers to page 150, "Match the Contestants with the Game Shows They Went on to Host"
1. Rudy Boesch, *Combat Missions*
2. Mark DeCarlo, *Studs* and *Big Deal*
3. Ron Maestri, *Quicksilver*
4. Frank Nicotero, *Street Smarts*
5. Mike Reilly, *Monopoly*
6. Paul Reubens, *You Don't Know Jack*
7. Gene Wood, *Beat the Clock* and *Anything You Can Do*

Answers to page 162, "Match the Celebrity with the Game Show She Appeared On"
1. Sandra Bernhard, *The $1.98 Beauty Show*
2. Vanna White, *The Price Is Right*
3. Kirstie Alley, *Password Plus*
4. Jenny Jones, *Press Your Luck*
5. Kathy Lee Gifford, *Name That Tune*
6. Meg Ryan, *The Price Is Right*

Answers to page 175, "Name the Seven *Playboy* Centerfolds Who Became Game Show Models and Who First Broke the Nudity Barrier"
Janice Pennington was the first to break the nudity barrier.
1. Julie Ciani was a model for *The Price Is Right*
2. Heather Kozar was a model for *The Price Is Right*
3. Jenny McCarthy was a co-host on *Singled Out*
4. Gena Lee Nolin was a model for *The Price Is Right*
5. Ann Pennington was an assistant on *Card Sharks*
6. Janice Pennington was a model for *The Price Is Right*
7. Nikki Ziering was a model for *The Price Is Right*

Bibliography

Anderson, Kent A. *Television Fraud: The History and Implications of the Quiz Show Scandals.* Westport, Conn.: Greenwood Press, 1978.

Barnouw, Erik. *A Tower in Babel: A History of Broadcasting in the United States.* Volume 1. New York: Oxford, 1966.

———. *The Golden Web: A History of Broadcasting in the United States.* Volume 2. New York: Oxford, 1968.

———. *The Image Empire: A History of Broadcasting in the United States.* Volume 3. New York: Oxford, 1970.

Barris, Chuck. *The Game Show King: A Confession.* New York: Carroll & Graf, 1993.

Blumenthal, Norman. *The TV Game Shows.* New York: Pyramid, 1975.

Broadcasting Magazine, Editors of. *The First Fifty Years of Broadcasting.* Washington, D.C.: Broadcasting Publications, 1982.

Brooks, Tim, and Earl Marsh. *The Complete Directory of Primetime Network TV Shows.* Sixth Edition. New York: Ballantine, 1995.

Brown, Les. *Les Brown's Encyclopedia of Television.* Third Edition. Detroit, Mich.: Visible Ink Press, 1992.

Buxton, Frank, and Bill Owen. *The Big Broadcast: 1920–1950.* New York: Flare Books/Avon Books, 1972.

Campbell, Robert. *The Golden Years of Broadcasting: A Celebration of the First Fifty Years of Radio and TV on NBC.* New York: Rutledge Book/Scribners, 1976.

Castleman, Harry, and Walter J. Podrazik. *Watching TV: Four Decades of American Television.* New York: McGraw-Hill, 1982.

———. *The TV Schedule Book: Four Decades of Network Programming from Sign-on to Sign-Off.* New York: McGraw-Hill, 1984.

David, Nina. *TV Season, 1974–1975.* Phoenix, Ariz.: Oryx Press, 1976.

———. *TV Season, 1975–1976.* Phoenix, Ariz.: Oryx Press, 1977.

———. *TV Season, 1976–1977.* Phoenix, Ariz.: Oryx Press, 1978.

————. *TV Season, 1977–1978.* Phoenix, Ariz.: Oryx Press, 1979.

DeLong, Thomas. *Quiz Craze: America's Infatuation with the Radio and Television Game Show.* Westport, Conn.: Praeger, 1991.

Downs, Hugh. *On Camera: My Ten Thousand Hours on Television.* New York: G.P. Putnam's Sons, 1986.

Duninng, John. *Tune in Yesterday: The Ultimate Encyclopedia of Old-Time Radio 1925–1976.* Englewood Cliffs, N.J.: Prentice-Hall, 1976.

Erickson, Hal. *Syndicated Television: The First Forty Years 1947–1987.* Jefferson, N.C.: McFarland & Company, 1989.

Fabe, Maxene. *TV Game Shows.* New York: Doubleday, 1979.

Fates, Gil. *What's My Line?: The Inside History of TV's Most Famous Panel Show.* Englewood Cliffs, N.J.: Prentice-Hall, 1978.

Fischer, Stuart. *Kid's TV: The First Twenty-five Years.* New York: Facts on File, Inc., 1983.

Goldenson, Leonard H., with Marvin J. Wolf. *Beating the Odds.* New York: Charles Scribner's Sons, 1991.

Grossman, Gary H. *Saturday Morning TV.* New York: Dell, 1981.

Hall, Monty, and Bill Libby. *Emcee Monty Hall.* New York: Ballantine, 1973.

Hyatt, Wesley. *The Encyclopedia of Daytime Television.* New York: Billboard Books, 1997.

Inman, David. *The TV Encyclopedia.* New York: Perigee Books, 1991.

Kaplan, Mike, ed., and Daily Variety. *Variety Who's Who in Show Business.* Revised Edition. New York: Garland Publishing, 1985.

Linkletter, Art, as told to George Bishop. *I Didn't Do It Alone: The Autobiography of Art Linkletter.* Ottawa, Ill.: Caroline House Publishers, 1980.

MacDonald, J. Fred. *One Nation under Television.* New York: Pantheon Books, 1990.

Marx, Groucho, with Hector Arce. *The Secret Word of Groucho.* New York: Berkeley Medallion Books, 1976.

McNeil, Alex. *Total Television: A Comprehensive Guide to Programming from 1948 to the Present.* Fourth Edition. New York: Penguin Books, 1996.

Norback, Craig T., and Norback Peter G., eds. *TV Guide Almanac.* New York: Ballantine Books, 1980.

O'Neill, Thomas. *The Emmys: Star Wars, Showdowns and the Supreme Test of TV's Best.* New York: Penguin Books, 1992.

Polizzi, Rick, and Fred Schaefer. *Spin Again: Board Games from the Fifties and Sixties.* San Francisco: Chronicle Books, 1991.

Ryan, Steve. *Classic Concentration: The Game, the Show, the Puzzles.* New York: Sterling Publishing, 1991.

Sackett, Susan. *Prime Time Hits: Television's Most Popular Network Programs 1950 to the Present.* New York: Billboard Books, 1993.

Sackett, Susan, and Cheryl Blythe. *You Can Be a Game Show Contestant and Win.* New York: Dell Books, 1982.

Sams, David R., and Robert L. Shook. *Wheel of Fortune.* New York: St. Martin's Press, 1987.

Shulman, Arthur, and Roger Youman. *How Sweet It Was; Television: A Pictorial Commentary.* New York: Bonanza Books, 1966.

Slater, Robert. *This ... Is CBS: A Chronicle of 60 Years.* Englewood Cliffs, N.J.: Prentice-Hall, 1988.

Slide, Anthony. *The Television Industry: A Historical Dictionary.* Westport, Conn.: Greenwood Press, 1991.

Stone, Joseph, and Tim Yohn. *Prime Time and Misdemeanors: Investigating the 1950's TV Quiz Scandal—a D.A.'s Account.* New Brunswick, N.J.: Rutgers University Press, 1992.

Tanerius, Steve. *How to Make a Fortune on TV Game Shows.* New York: Zebra Books, 1987.

Terrace, Vincent. *Television, 1970–1980.* San Diego: A.S. Barnes and Company, 1981.

———. *Encyclopedia of TV Series, Pilots and Specials 1974–1984.* New York: Baseline, 1985.

———. *Encyclopedia of TV Series, Pilots and Specials, 1937–1973.* New York: New York Zoetrope, 1986.

————. *Fifty Years of Television: A Guide to Series and Pilots, 1937–1988.* New York: Cornwall Books, 1991.

Trebek, Alex, and Peter Barsocchini. *The Jeopardy! Book.* New York: HarperCollins, 1990.

Whitburn, Joel. *Top Page Singles 1955–1990.* Menomonee Falls, Wis.: Record Research, 1991.

Winship, Michael. *Television.* New York: Random House, 1988.

Woolery, George. *Children's Television: The First Thirty-five Years, 1946–1981. Part II: Live, Film and Tape Series.* Metuchen, N.J.: Scarecrow Press, 1985.

Magazines
Billboard Magazine
Broadcasting Magazine
Daily Variety
Electronic Media
Hollywood Reporter
Spin Again Magazine
Television Forecast
Television Index
TV Guide
TV-Radio Age
TV-Radio Daily
TV-Radio Life
Variety

Almanacs
International Television Almanac
Quigley Publications, New York
Radio Annual, Television Yearbook
Radio Daily Television Daily

Newspapers
Bergen Record, New Jersey
Chicago Tribune
Las Vegas Sun
Los Angeles Daily News
Los Angeles Herald Examiner
Los Angeles Times
New York Daily News
New York Post
New York Times

Acknowledgments

The authors would like to thank the following people, production companies, networks, and photo services for helping us gather the information and pictures used in this book.

ABC television, ABR Entertainment, Ginger Adams, Art Alisi, Marty Allen, Stephanie Allen, Paul Alter, Ralph Andrews Productions, Kathleen Ankers, George Ansbro, Bill Armstrong, Associated Press, Portia Badham, Ron Baldwin, Bob Barker, Barbara Barnard, Chuck Barris Productions, Barry and Enright Productions, Jack Barry, Shirley Bawidamann, Orson Bean, Mark Becker, Joe Behar, John Behrens, Ellie Bendes, Bern Bennett, Lisa Berg, Peter Berlin, Mike Bevan, Stu Billett, Dennis Biondi, Blair Entertainment, Leona Blair, Howard Blumenthal, Caroline Bock, Bob Boden, Lin Bolen, Phyllis Borea, Mark Bowerman, Frank Bresee, Michael Brockman, Richard Brockway, Fred Bronson, Jean De Vivier Brown, Buena Vista Television, Gloria Burke, Anne Burkhimer, Kevin Burns, CBA Television, California State University—Northridge, Charles Cappleman, Bill Carruthers, Johnny Carson, Randall Carver, Joe Cates, Heidi Cayn, Century Towers Productions, Bill Chastain, Norman Checkor, Roxanne Checkor, Erik Christensen, Dick Clark, Gail Clark, Jack Clark, Mike Clark, Bob Clayton, Cleveland Press, Yoko Coleman, Columbia Pictures Television, Brian Conn, Ted Cooper, Grover Crisp, Rich Cronin, Dan Cross, Ann Cullen, Bill Cullen, Jean Cummings, Dresser Dahlstead, Kay Daly, Michael Davies, Richard Dawson, Lisa Dee, Milton DeLugg, Phyllis Diller, The Disney Channel, Roger Dobkowitz, Phil Donahue, Don Pitts Voices, Doodlebug, Dick Dudley, Geoff Edwards, Ralph Edwards Productions, Dan Einstein, Dan Enright, Susan Epstein, Frank Esopi, Joyce Estrin, Bob Eubanks, George Faber, Gil Fates, Chester Feldman, George Fennaman, Rob Fiedler, Art Fleming, Michael Fleming, Ed Flesh, Rex Fluty, Jr., Food Network, Four Star Entertainment, Dan Fox, Sonny Fox, Ladd Framer, Howard Frank, Steve Friedman, Ester Furst, Game Show Network, Lloyd Gaynes, Alan Gilbert, Johnny Gilbert, Michale Gilman, Pat Gleason, Andrew Golder, Jeff Goldstein, Jonathan Goodson, Mark Goodson, Frank Gorshin, Berni Gould, Chet Gould, Charlene Grayson, Ron Greenberg, Don Gregory, Merv Griffin, Merv Griffin Productions, Darris Gringeri, John Guedel, Michael Gwartney, Monty Hall, Ed Hammond, Lon Harding, John Harlan, Ron Harris, William Harris, Stefan Hatos, Michael Hawks, Merrill Heatter, Franklin Heller, Art Hellyer, Kay Henley, Marilu Henner, Shelley Herman, Mike Hill, Bill Hillier, Bob Hilton, Howard Hinderstein, Donna Holden, Larry Hovis, Wayne Howell, Tina Hummel, Barbara Hunter, Marty Ingels, Jerita Ingle, Dan Ingram, Stacy Jackson (Lifetime Television), Frank Jacoby, Chris Jacquish, Art James, Dennis James, Bert Jayasekera, Allan Jeffreys, Jim Victory Television, Gabrielle Johnston, Romain Johnston, Gary Jonke, Ed Jubert, KCAL-TV, KCOP-TV, KMPC Radio, KRLA Radio, KTLA-TV, KTTV-TV, Rick Kates,

Harris Katleman, Cynthia Kazarian, Mary Kellogg, Bob Kennedy, Tom Kennedy, Richard Kline, King World, Allan Koss, Jerry Kupcinet, Jim Lange, Richard Lawrence, Vicki Lawrence-Schultz, Steve LeBlang, Jean Lewis, Frank Liberman, Library of Congress, Charles Lisanby, Lorimar-Telepictures, Delilah Loud, Glenn Lowney, Allen Ludden, MTV Networks, Sue MacIntyre, Dave Mackey, Sheila MacRae, Rose Marie, Lori Marshall, Peter Marshall, Sandy Martindale, Wink Martindale, Nick Marino, Perry Massey, Mark Maxwell-Smith, Phillip Mayer, Bill McCord, Joel McGee, Paul McGuire, Matt McKenzie, Jim McKrell, Carol Merrill, Mike Metzger, David Michaels, Jennifer Michaels, Ann Miller, Jonathan Miller (Television Index), James Monaco, Jaye P. Morgan, Don Morrow, Gregg Moscoe, Roger Muir, John Mula, Jan Murray, Museum of TV and Radio, Russ Myerson NBC Television, Dave Nagel (ESPN), Jack Narz, Mike Narz, Jim Newton, Marilyn Nicholson, Robert Noah, Charlie O'Donnell, Odyssey Channel, Karen Osmer, Matt Ottinger, Gary Owens, Betsy Palmer, Betty Panos, Don Pardo, Lillian Parker, Marty Pasetta, Dolly Pearl, Jim Peck, Erin Perry, Jim Perry, Personality Photos, Inc., Susan Petracca, Chuck Pharis, Stuart Phelps, Don Pitts, Gail Pitts, Playboy Enterprises, Beverly Pomerantz, Steve Radosh, Mark Ragonese, Gene Rayburn, Reeves Entertainment, Don Reid, Richard Reid, Charles Nelson Reilly, John Rhinehart, Ray Richmond, Geraldo Rivera, Joan Rivers, Brian Robinette, Rod Roddy, Cindy Ronzoni, Heidi Rothbart, Michele Roth, Cathi Ryan, Saban Productions, Anthony Sabatino, Pat Sajak, Soupy Sales, Theresa Savage, George Schlatter, David Schwartz, Murray Schwartz, Screen Gems Television, Jeremy Shamos, Stephanie Sheeran, Frances Siddon, K. Mathy Simon, Ron Simon, Susan Simons, Nancy Sinatra, Ira Skutch, Bill Smith, Lillian M. Smith, Alan Solomon, Aaron Solomon, David Sparks, Pamm Spencer, Susan Stafford, Robert Stahl, Willie Stein, Herb Stemple, Scott Sternberg, Bob Stewart, Bob Stewart Productions, Jay Stewart, Sande Stewart, Bunny Stivers, Mike Stokey, Scott Stone, Stone-Stanley Productions, Ralph Story, Milt Suchin, Marc Summers, Mark Surface, Bob Synes, Syracuse University, Joel Tator, Jake Taubert, Lori Teliez, Lloyd Thaxton, Geoff Theobald, Alan Thicke, Peter Tomarken, Alex Trebek, Ryan Tredinnik, Tom Trimble, 20th Century-Fox Television, UCLA, UPS, USA Cable Network, USC Archives, Jack Vackrinos, Marge Van Ostrand, Viacom, Lee Vines, Keenie Voigt, WABC-TV, WNEW-TV, WPIX-TV, WQED-TV, WWOR-TV, Richard Wagoner, Waldwick High School, Dale Walsh, Phillip Wayne, Harfield Weedin, Bill Wendell, Adam West, Randy West, Betty White, Paul Winchell, William Patterson College, Dave Willinger, Nancy Wolfson, Jay Wolpert, Gene Wood Worldvision, Chuck Woolery, Irene Wostbrock.

About the Authors

Steve Ryan

If the world's greatest magician was Harry Houdini, and the world's greatest detective was Sherlock Holmes, then surely the world's greatest puzzle and game master is Steve Ryan, recognized as one of the most prolific creators of puzzles in the world, with more than 12,000 brain-busting bafflers to his credit. This virtuoso of vexation has been inventing games and puzzles since childhood. Early in his career he found a market for his creations at Copley News Service, where his "Puzzles & Posers" and "Zig-Zag" features have appeared for more than twenty-five years.

Ryan's creative genius also catapulted him into television, where he co-created and developed the TV game show *Blockbusters* for television's most prestigious game show packager, Mark Goodson. Ryan has also written for *Password Plus, Trivia Trap, Body Language,* and *Catch Phrase,* and he created all the rebus puzzles for TV's *Classic Concentration* and contributed *The Price Is Right* pricing game "Now & Then."

Currently, Ryan is senior games executive at Goodson's lottery division where he creates games with million-dollar payoffs for state lottery game shows, including *The Big Spin* in California. And, Steve's rebus creations are back and more exciting than ever in the Bally Gaming "Concentration" slot machine.

Ryan is the author of more than twenty popular books, including *Brain Busters, Lunchbox Puzzles, Sit & Solve Pencil Puzzles, Test Your Puzzle IQ, Mystifying Math Puzzles, Great Rebus Puzzles,* and *Classic Concentration,* and he is co-author of *The Encyclopedia of TV Game Shows.* His puzzles have also appeared in such magazines as *Games, Nickelodeon,* and *World of Puzzles* in the United States and *Games & Puzzles* in the United Kingdom. Worldwide, his puzzle books have been translated into Chinese, Dutch, French, Italian, Portuguese, Russian, and Spanish and have also surfaced in India, Pakistan, and Indonesia with other faraway lands soon to experience Ryan's puzzling world.

Many predicted Ryan's gifts in art, design, and mathematics would lead to a career in architecture. But as usual, Ryan had a surprise twist in store: He built a mental gymnastics empire instead.

Nothing puzzling about that.

For more information visit: www.SteveRyanGames.com.

Fred Wostbrock

One of the leading historians of game shows, Wostbrock has been a game show fan since the age of sixteen when in 1976 he attended his first game show taping in New York City and met the legendary Bill Cullen and game show creator Bob Stewart. For the next two years Wostbrock was a frequent visitor to many episodes of *The $20,000 Pyramid* and *The $25,000 Pyramid.* In 1978 Wostbrock attended numerous tapings of *Pass the Buck,* once again starring the legendary Bill Cullen and created by Bob Stewart. Wostbrock will always remember joining Bill Cullen and Bob Stewart backstage for lunch. It was during that lunch that Wostbrock had the pleasure of speaking at length to both Bill Cullen and Bob Stewart about the shows they worked on together from *The Price Is Right, Eye Guess, You're Putting Me On, Three on a Match, Winning Streak, Blankety Blanks,* and *The $25,000 Pyramid* to *Pass the Buck.*

A graduate of Syracuse University, Wostbrock majored in television broadcasting and communication law. Since moving to Los Angeles in 1982, he has worked on more than ten national network and syndicated game shows. In the summer of 1987, he co-produced a five-part special on the history of game shows with Wink Martindale for *Good Morning America.*

Wostbrock has been featured on *E!, Entertainment Tonight, Good Morning America, A&E Biography, NBC News,* and *ABC News.* He also has guest starred on *Donahue, Geraldo, The Late Show, Marilu, The Joan Rivers Show,* and *Rolanda.* In 2002 and 2003 Wostbrock helped book two weeks of *Hollywood Squares* as they featured many of his clients as they saluted America's favorite game show emcees.

In 1990, Cynthia Kazarian, Pamela Spencer, and Don Pitts welcomed Fred to their successful agency as a game show, infomercial, and celebrity agent. In 1995, the agency was renamed Kazarian Spencer and Associates, and Wostbrock currently works in Studio City, California. Among his clients are giants in the game show world, from America's favorite emcees to Emmy-winning creators to television's favorite celebrity and film icons. Wostbrock is also pleased to work with the estates of Bill Cullen, Allen Ludden, and Gene Rayburn.

From 2000 to 2003, Wostbrock interviewed game show giants Bob Barker, Monty Hall, and Bob Stewart for the TV Academy. Each interview was researched to perfection and took four hours. The interviews were highlighted in *Emmy* magazine.

Wostbrock possesses the largest collection of game show memorabilia and rare game show photos in the United States.

We hope you have enjoyed *The Ultimate TV Game Show Book.* If you would like contribute to a future volume, submit your entry to ultimatetvlists@aol.com. We can't respond personally to all submissions, but we will include your name on the acknowledgments page if your proposal is unique, accurate, and original. Thank you for being as fanatical about game shows as we are.

Index